"Steve Gerali's book provides a thoughtful, issue that has been marked by silence. This b while striking a powerful blow to the fears concerning masturbation. A book to be read and discussed by men and women of all ages."

BRUCE SPERLING, *youth pastor, Lombard, Illinois*

"Steve has written an engaging book that reveals his candor as a truth-teller and his humility as a truth-seeker. I'm grateful that he has applied both his wisdom and courage to writing about such a critical issue as masturbation."

DR. DAVE RAHN, *director, Huntington College's Link Institute; vice president, YFC/USA Ministries*

"Steve Gerali's insights will be helpful in allowing young men and women to take a journey of discerning God's will for their lives in regard to this issue. As a youth pastor, I have been praying for a book that will help my students process through this wisdom issue—I found it!"

NEIL GATTEN, *youth minister, Scottsdale, Arizona*

"After dealing with this sensitive issue for more than twenty years in youth ministry, I am thrilled to have a fresh, grounded, and insightful book that puts this issue into perspective. *The Struggle* not only addresses the myths associated with this topic but also presents some biblical guidelines that should prove to be helpful for many."

SUE MYERS, *pastor to youth, Trinity Bible Church, Phoenix, Arizona*

"If you're like me and not satisfied with the 'because I said so' answer, then this book may be an eye-opener into what has formed our beliefs and culture. This book can give youth workers wisdom regarding the issue of masturbation, regardless of his or her personal theology."

JOSHUA HIGGINS, *youth pastor*

Go   Ahead:

TH1NK: *about God*
about life
about others

Faith isn't just an act; it's something you live—something huge and sometimes unimaginable. By getting into the real issues in your life, TH1NK books open opportunities to talk honestly about your faith, your relationship with God and others, as well as all the things life throws at you.

Don't let other people th1nk for you . . .

TH1NK for yourself.

www.th1nkbooks.com

I CAN'T TALK ABOUT THIS.

LET'S BE HONEST,
EVERY GUY
STRUGGLES
WITH IT.

тHе STRuGGLE
STEVE GERALI

WHAT DOES THE
BIBLE SAY ABOUT IT?

ARE YOU SERIOUS?

TH1NK Books
an imprint of NavPress®

NAVPRESS
P.O. Box 35001
Colorado Springs, CO 80935

The Navigators is an international Christian organization. Our mission is to reach, disciple, and equip people to know Christ and to make Him known through successive generations. We envision multitudes of diverse people in the United States and every other nation who have a passionate love for Christ, live a lifestyle of sharing Christ's love, and multiply spiritual laborers among those without Christ.

NavPress is the publishing ministry of The Navigators. NavPress publications help believers learn biblical truth and apply what they learn to their lives and ministries. Our mission is to stimulate spiritual formation among our readers.

ISBN 1-57683-455-7

Cover Images: DigitalVision
Cover Design: David Carlson Design
Creative Team: Jay Howver, Gary Wilde, Nat Akin, Darla Hightower, Glynese Northam

Some of the anecdotal illustrations in this book are true to life and are included with the permission of the persons involved. All other illustrations are composites of real situations, and any resemblance to people living or dead is coincidental.

Unless otherwise identified, all Scripture quotations in this publication are taken from the HOLY BIBLE: NEW INTERNATIONAL VERSION® (NIV®). Copyright © 1973, 1978, 1984 by International Bible Society. Used by permission of Zondervan Publishing House. All rights reserved. Other versions used include: the *New American Standard Bible* (NASB), © The Lockman Foundation 1960, 1962, 1963, 1968, 1971, 1972, 1973, 1975, 1977; and the *New Revised Standard Version* (NRSV), copyright © 1989, by the Division of Christian Education of the National Council of the Churches of Christ in the USA, used by permission, all rights reserved.

Gerali, Steve.
    The struggle / by Steve Gerali.-- 1st ed.
      p. cm.
Includes bibliographical references and index.
    ISBN 1-57683-455-7
    1. Masturbation--Religious aspects--Christianity. 2. Christian
teenagers--Religious life. I. Title.
    BT708.5.G47 2003
    241'.66--dc22
                                        2003014484

Printed in Canada

1 2 3 4 5 6 7 8 9 10 / 07 06 05 04 03

FOR A FREE CATALOG OF
NAVPRESS BOOKS & BIBLE STUDIES,
CALL 1-800-366-7788 (USA)
OR 1-416-499-4615 (CANADA)

"As iron sharpens iron, so one man sharpens another"

This book is dedicated to the men that I have had the privilege of being in a mentoring relationship with. Their honesty with struggles, openness to talk about issues, and fervent desire to lead a life of integrity with Jesus Christ have helped to make me "sharper" and formulate the context of this book.

CONTENTS

WATCH OUT FOR THAT ARMORED TANK!

I became a man on a mission. Before this little conversation ended, I was determined that youth-pastor Matt would say the word out loud.

I was talking with Matt about an upcoming youth retreat. I'd be spending an entire evening discussing adolescent sexuality with the parents, followed by a weekend of sessions with their teenagers. Matt had just come from a meeting with his Parent Advisory Team, and he called me to talk about expectations.

"Steve, our parents want to know how to help their kids discern sexual messages in the media and culture while developing a healthy, biblical view of sexuality," he said. "Will that be in your presentation?"

"I think I could cover that."

"We're also expecting you to help parents coach their teens about establishing dating guidelines. Some parents want you to answer the question of 'How far is too far?' Can you do that?" he asked.

"I'll work that in too."

"And many parents asked about how to address various other issues, such as oral sex, homosexuality, contraception, abstinence, sexual peer pressure, and modest dress from a biblical perspective. What about that?" he said.

"Well, if we have the time, I can approach those topics too."

Then he said, "They *really* want you to address other topics of sexuality as well."

I was caught off guard. This peaked my curiosity. I had a hunch that I could figure out where this conversation was going. I also realized that Matt would have a more difficult time talking about the "other topic."

"What other issues of sexuality do you mean, Matt?"

"Well . . . ah, lust and other related issues."

"Other lust-related issues?" I asked. "Like what, Matt?"

"You know . . . lust . . . uh . . . especially as it relates to guys."

At this point, I rather cruelly decided to play a little dumb and see how far Matt would go before he actually had to utter the word.

"I'm not sure what sexual issue you're talking about, Matt."

"You know . . . the *Big M!*" He was trying to keep it lighthearted, though I could feel him sweating through the phone lines.

"The Big M?" I asked in a puzzled voice. "Do you mean *menstruation?*"

"No," he said with a chuckle. I waited to see if he would say anything more, but he didn't.

"*Marriage?*"

"No," he said, and I detected rising frustration.

I paused again, and this time the silence was uncomfortably long. He didn't say a word.

"You can't mean *menopause*. Most teenagers aren't interested in menopause, unless some of the moms want me to help their teens understand what they're going through. Living with a mother going through menopause can be tough for a teen."

I rambled on until, rather exasperated, Matt interrupted. "No, Steve, not menopause . . . They want you to talk about . . . umm . . . masturbation."

Just the way he said the word sounded as if it were truly filthy.

Had he indeed spoken the vilest of all perversions? Had he entered into the forbidden zone of sexual wickedness? Had all the forces of hell been unleashed, summoned, and empowered for battle because the unspeakable evil was suddenly spoken aloud?

Were we both in danger of being run over by a speeding armored tank sent straight from the heavenly throne of judgment, just because the word had finally been uttered?

TOUGH TO TALK ABOUT "IT"

No tank had crashed through my office wall—yet—so I asked Matt why the word *masturbation* was so difficult for him to say.

"I guess I just feel embarrassed talking about it because it's so shaming. At least that's the way I was raised. I was always taught that Christians shouldn't even talk about such things."

How about you? Can you relate? Whether your experience is

similar to Matt's or not, I believe you've picked up this book because you've experienced some struggle with masturbation. Either you've struggled with embarrassment and shame in talking about it, or wrestled with forming a view about it, or grappled with your conscience after masturbating.

Whatever the case, whatever the pressing questions on your mind, you're going to find some solid answers in the pages ahead. So I invite you to read on.

For the past eight years I've taught a Human Sexuality course at a Christian college. When I ask students where they learned about sexual issues and values, they usually point to their homes—but their homes were and are silent about masturbation. Occasionally guys will say that their parents said something like "Don't do *that.*" Or their fathers may have said, "Don't do that . . . *too much.*" But the issue is typically left on the back burner.

When asked about how their churches treated the subject, students will usually say that either it was never talked about or that it was briefly raised under the heading of *lust.* Many church leaders believe they're openly discussing the issue when they simply parrot timeworn ideas they've heard from others; but most of the time those concepts never directly engage the issue of masturbation. These ideologies, which we'll discuss later, raise more questions and breed more anxiety about masturbation than anything else! In short, the blanket of silence is still there, but those leaders have pinned pat answers to the subject. In other words, the church hasn't helped us much in formulating a *biblically and culturally informed personal view* of masturbation.

Is this shaming, binding blanket of silence too thick to penetrate?

No. The starting point is simply to admit that masturbation is a difficult and uncomfortable subject. In fact, when I originally met for lunch with the representatives from NavPress to present my vision for this book, we found the discomfort . . . well, discomforting. Try having a serious discussion about masturbation in a crowded restaurant! It feels as if the entire establishment can hear every word you're saying. We were constantly, stealthily looking around to see if anyone was listening. And the conversation always stopped when our waitress approached. She had to be wondering what kind of espionage we were planning.

Admittedly, it is difficult to talk about masturbation. It certainly has been uncomfortable for me to tell certain people about the subject of this book. I called my wife back in Chicago after I finished my meeting with NavPress in Colorado Springs. She knew I was talking to the editors about an entirely different book. After I told her that I was going to be writing on masturbation, her immediate response was, "What are you going to tell your parents when they ask about this book?"

Wow! I hadn't thought about that. What would *you* say? Regardless of your age, it's weird talking to your parents about anything sexual, let alone masturbation. I thought it over for a moment.

"I'll tell them I'm writing a 'current-issue' book for youth."

REMEMBER: THIS IS A "TH1NK BOOK"

One of my goals in these pages is to deal with masturbation in a way that generates critical thought and dialogue. That's what the TH1NK books are all about, so I'm going to ask you to seriously engage your brain as you read. I've found that when people deal with this topic in a God-honoring manner, they find a kind of spiritual relief, regardless of their eventual conclusions. They gain freedom to engage the topic of masturbation, and sexuality in general, without the old fear, guilt, and shame. I trust that this book facilitates a "permission to speak," so that you can discuss this subject, think it through, and eventually formulate a biblically and culturally informed personal viewpoint.

Being informed involves thinking through the issues in a critical manner—and critical thought means approaching the subject without embarrassment. It means that we can call on all of the truth that God reveals through His Word, through the sciences, and through history. It also means that we agree to approach the subject with a spirit intent on finding truth without judgment. We agree to be part of the process instead of a hindrance to it. We agree to create a safe environment so that those who wrestle with this issue can openly do so.

The subject of masturbation has to be approached *biblically*, but also *culturally*. That's because popular culture has taken the lead away from the church by openly dealing with masturbation in printed media, music, and movies. Past generations have conveyed dogmatic views about masturbation that proved to be built on errors and lies. As these myths have been exposed, the generation that followed became more skeptical about what it believed. A growing mistrust over authoritative stances made many leaders timid about dealing with the issue.

By the beginning of the twentieth century there were so many myths, misconceptions, and false teachings—as well as so much confusion, guilt, shame, ignorance, and embarrassment—that the church retreated from its openly dogmatic views to take a "no talk" stance about masturbation. Our understanding of these cultural variables as they developed from generation to generation will give us a clearer understanding of where we are today.

After all, values are passed and tweaked from generation to generation. Things that were valued three generations ago are seen differently by the generation of today. This phenomenon of transforming certain values so that their application is current is called the pursuit of *cultural relevance*. These generational shifts and changes often leave us questioning the conclusions and applications of the past. For example, if I were to say that bowling is morally wrong, many people today would wonder what planet I was from. Yet just three generations ago bowling was a highly controversial pastime. (In fact, as youth pastor twenty-five years ago, I remember coming under fire from some elderly saints when I planned an all-night bowling event for teens.)

When I spoke to a friend about this book, he raised his eyebrow and commented that I may no longer be asked to speak in certain churches because I am the author of a book about . . . he lowered his voice to a whisper: "Masturbation." He's probably right. But it is my prayer that this book will defeat Satan's tactics and open the doors to healthy, God-honoring dialogue about such a burdensome issue for many men and women who want to live in God's will.

I pray that you'll walk with me through those open doors and read the book with an open heart. Invite the Holy Spirit to use each chapter as a tool to teach, guide, and direct you. I want to help you formulate a biblical and cultural personal view about masturbation, but the Spirit is your ultimate teacher. I simply ask: *Reserve your decision about whether masturbation is right or wrong for you until you have read the entire book.*

THE GOAL IS FREEDOM

Once you've read the book—no matter your final conclusion—you will be a freer person. I just know it.

Some years ago, I spoke at a certain church in Michigan that had sponsored an event on understanding teenagers. After my talk, one father asked about the role of masturbation in an adolescent male's life. I didn't want to get into the issue. So I gave a short and vague response, hoping the questioner would be satisfied.

He wasn't; he kept pressing. Before I realized what was happening, some of the other men in the room began to ask deeper questions, and we were in the middle of a full-blown discussion. It was there that I outlined some of the material that we will cover in this book.

Now, here's the thing: In the middle of the room sat the senior pastor of this large conservative church, along with his wife. He fixed his gaze on me and didn't blink. I recall thinking that any minute he was going to stand up and yell, *"Heretic!"* Then there would be a public burning in the church parking lot.

At the end of the session the pastor did approach me. "May I speak to you, please . . . in my office?" he asked.

"Sure," I replied, hoping for the best—that I'd merely be barred from speaking at his church again.

He opened his office door and allowed me to enter ahead of him. Then he closed the door behind him and leaned back against it. I remembered thinking, *Now I'm trapped!*

Suddenly this stern-looking man's countenance changed. He proceeded to tell me that he had masturbated from the time that he was twelve years old until after college, when he got married. He always assumed this was one of the worst sins he could commit. "Steve, I've thought that everything that went wrong in my life, ministry, or marriage was the result of years of 'practicing this sin,' and that I had lost favor with God."

He went on to quote Galatians 6:7-8: "Do not be deceived: God cannot be mocked. A man reaps what he sows. The one who sows to please his sinful nature, from that nature will reap destruction; the one who sows to please the Spirit, from the Spirit will reap eternal life." This pastor was convinced that he was paying for his masturbation when anything at all went wrong in his life. He struggled for years to come to some kind of resolution—but he never could . . . until that morning . . . during that session. Until then, *he'd lived under the constant fear that a heavenly tank would take him out at any moment.*

Yet as he told me his story, he began to cry tears of joy.

Why? What had he learned within such a short time on this Saturday morning? How had his heart changed and his relationship with God transformed?

You want to know the answers to those questions, right? And I hope your own heart is burning with your own questions and longing for your own answers. That's how "the struggle" will actually become a holy adventure for you. We'll trek together with Bible in hand down through ancient history and into modern culture. Answers will arise as we burrow deep into a topic that for too long has remained buried under layer upon layer of shame.

Are you ready to begin digging? We'll dig deep and talk openly without fear of the armored tank that never comes, because it doesn't exist.

STEVE GERALI

CHAPTER ONE

STILL STRUGGLING IN SILENCE?

"I can't keep dealing with this horrible sin in my life," Kyle
blurted.
The look of pain in his eyes melted my heart.

I stood before the group of animated high schoolers as they fired
off questions about the Bible and real life. Did I say I was standing?
More to the point, I was sitting on the hot seat. You see, it didn't take
these hormone-driven teens long to raise the topic of sexuality.

I'd been doing just fine with "How can you tell when you've found
the right girl?" and "What's the best way to break up with a guy?" But
then one of the students raised his hand . . . and lowered the boom: "Is
it a sin to masturbate?"

Silence.

It's not something you ask in public, right? The apparently
"unspeakable" had been uttered, yet deep down I knew most of the kids
in the room had secretly wanted to raise the question. I proceeded to
answer, openly and honestly.

After our Q & A session ended, a number of students surrounded
me, still asking questions about masturbation. One of the guys standing in this small circle suddenly became aware of the group's open discussion and commented, "I can't believe we're talking about this . . . *in*
church!"

Could you have said the same? That is, have you noticed that masturbation is the silent skeleton in the church's closet? It's always been a difficult subject for the church. Yet, with our advance into the twenty-first century, popular culture has brought virtually everything sexual into the light of day—for better or worse. Today, you can find masturbation openly treated in numerous settings, from middle-school curriculums to pop music. Despite this, we Christians still shy away from the issue. It's as if a dark cloud of silence still overshadows the "M" word for us.

But isn't it time to break the silence? Isn't it time to start talking about a once unmentionable taboo?

"We never talk about sex in my house. I don't think my parents even know about masturbation." —Lisa, 17

WHAT DOES THE SILENCE TELL YOU?

Students in my Human Sexuality courses claim they learned about masturbation mainly through their friends, their experience of it, or the media. But are these the most credible or authoritative sources? Especially when it comes to information passing "through the grapevine," we might be wise to ask whether the grapevine has any root rot, making the info a bit suspect.

Again, we face silence from more potentially trustworthy sources. And silence creates an insecurity often handed down from generation to generation. So what is the silence saying to you these days? Here are two of the big messages a lot of people are hearing:

1. The Silence says, "I'm committing a big-time evil—the worst." Do you believe it? Were you told not to touch yourself as a child? That parts of your body were "dirty"? Did you hear jokes about masturbation as a preteen—with punch lines that made it sound like the ultimate perversion?

If you're like me, you received dogmatic messages that masturbation is grossly sinful from a verbal minority who rarely offered concrete biblical support for their pronouncements. These folks were never challenged to think critically, which includes thinking theologically about the issue. So they left in their wake many young men struggling alone, feeling evil, guilty, ashamed, and defeated.

"No one talked about it when I was in junior high and high school, so I thought nobody else did it. I thought I was so evil."   **—Jake, 20**

The president of the college where I formerly taught once received a letter from a concerned parent whose son had sat in on my Human Sexuality class. It happened to be the day we were talking about masturbation. The letter rebuked the college, the president, and me for compromising our Christian integrity. "I can't believe a Christian college would even allow a discussion on such a topic in its classrooms," he wrote. "I would never let my son attend such a school." He ranked masturbation among the vilest of evils, so wicked that it violated the sacredness of the classrooms at a Christian school.

No wonder we struggle! The silence tells us that masturbation is a contemptible depravity, yet almost every man admits to personal involvement in it. (Those who don't admit to it—are they telling the truth?)

2. The Silence says, "I'm the only guy in the world who's doing it." Kyle figured he was that one. This college sophomore called me one afternoon asking if he could come in and talk. When he arrived at my office he radiated pure agony.

"I can't keep dealing with this horrible sin in my life," he blurted. After I got him settled down a bit, he told me of his struggles with masturbation. He may not have thought he was the only guy doing it, but he definitely believed he struggled more than any other person alive. "I'm sure you've never seen a problem like this before," he said.

It seems the dorm guys around him typically spoke of masturbation as if it were never a problem. Others became super pious, doubtful that so heinous a sin could overtake a real Christian. Or they just clammed up and moved on to other things.

Kyle had also developed some pretty potent fears, something not all that unusual. Consider three of the "fear factors" that often kick in when sexual guilt and shame ratchet up to unbearable levels.

Fear Factor #1: Get ready, your judgment day's a-comin'! As a young teen, Kyle didn't know what masturbation was until he began touching himself one day while he was taking a shower. Later, he felt so guilty that he couldn't even talk about it to his closest friend. Eventually, he came to believe that because he wasn't delivered from this struggle through prayer, God had turned away from him.

We often forget that Satan is the great accuser. He accuses the saints in order to isolate, immobilize, and defeat them. Satan accomplished that in this young man's life. Kyle even began to think he was beyond God's grace, as certain folks in his church said masturbation was an act of blasphemy against the Holy Spirit. It was therefore unpardonable.

The result: a young man living under the constant fear of impending doom. *When will the axe of divine judgment fall on me?* Kyle thought. Actor Roy Scheider captured the feeling when he envisioned his own death scene: "I imagine myself in my eighties, seeing a girl with gorgeous legs on the other side of the street. I start to follow her, step off the curb without looking, and get hit by a truck." Is it really our fate to be suddenly wiped out because of our sexual desire?

As you probably know, it can seem that way.

Judgment also flows from those who vigorously announce their repulsion. One young lady stridently questioned me after a sexuality class: "That's so gross and disgusting; why would anyone do *that*?" Not too many guys are going to talk about masturbation after such a comment. So, once again, we crawl back under the judging, shaming blanket of silence.

Fear Factor #2: What if you're suddenly "outed," buddy? Gotcha! It's the terror of being discovered. But why such horror? It's pretty widely known that most men masturbate, the statistics claiming up to 97 percent of us. (As I hinted earlier, many who interpret such stats also add that the other 3 percent are lying. We might laugh at this, but in reality, some men never experience masturbation. Statistics also reveal that about 40 percent of all women masturbate.)

Nevertheless, you may live in the fear that somebody might find out about *you!* Suppose somebody (like your mom, girlfriend, or a leader you respect) asks, "Do *YOU* masturbate?" Then you may combat the fear of being discovered by putting on your trusty camouflage persona. You keep your mouth shut, take a low profile in the unfolding conversation, and act somewhat disinterested in order to throw off any suspicions. You know the conversation will eventually end and you may, with any luck, dodge the painful bullets of honest communication and keep the emotional bloodletting to a minimum.

We just don't want to be outed. Let the issue be some other guy's problem; we'll view it all from afar. Critical thought and honest conversation? No thanks. Cookie-cutter concepts and trite clichés? Bring 'em on. After all, why get close to an issue that carries so much personal shame?

"My dad talked about it really quickly; he just said it's natural. But if you think about a girl, it's wrong."   —Brian, 22

Fear Factor #3: Suppose you really have no idea how to think about all this? This is the fear of ignorance, potentially leading to public embarrassment. Lots of guys remain silent because they haven't developed a point of view on the matter. They haven't yet formulated a solid, personal stance built on historical and biblical truth. Once again Satan keeps many of us in bondage because what little knowledge we have has been shaped by damning comments and secondhand information from unreliable sources.

It's amazing that the two strongest value-forming institutions in the Christian's life—the home and church—generate the most fear about this topic. They're primarily responsible for the thick wall of silence when, ironically, they should be freeing young men to experience heartfelt conviction rather than false guilt, freedom rather than bondage, and safety rather than shame. This will only happen if both institutions determine to create a safe place and allow guys to be *informed*, culturally and biblically.

WHAT IS YOUR CULTURE SAYING?

Imagine the benefit if we were to overcome the discomfort of candid discussion about masturbation, openly engaging with Scripture and culture as we've done in the past with other sexual issues. In the past the church only talked about sex as a means for procreation. To even acknowledge any pleasure in it was perverted. Today there are many Christian books written about pleasure in marital sex. Many Christians openly admit to sex in marriage as a means for pleasure.

We can do it again. The silence is breakable.

First let's admit that the popular culture today delivers a truckload of misconceptions without challenge. Yet if we Christians don't know the culture then we can't combat it, especially if it doesn't jibe with biblical standards.

Where to begin our education? Suppose we start with the popular vernacular for masturbation. Here's where I routinely invite parents and youth leaders into an exercise that confronts their uneasiness, that reminds them of the down-to-earth slang of the day. I put people on teams. Then I present the entire group with a sexual topic like masturbation. The teams have three minutes to jot every word or phrase they've ever heard to describe that topic.

Now, the scoring isn't at all fancy: The team with the most entries wins. And it's amazing what the competitive spirit will do to a group's inhibitions. It immediately hurtles them past the discomfort of talking about sexual issues, because about two minutes into this game everybody focuses with wild-eyed enthusiasm on attaining the coveted thrill of victory. No, winning isn't everything. But the prospect of winning sure loosens the tongue.

When the fierce battle is over and we're debriefing the action, often people will comment that they heard a particular term but didn't know that it referred to a sexual act. Or maybe they didn't know many of the slang or technical terms at all. One mother told me she'd been innocently using a sexual slang term in the family for years—with no clue as to its "other" meaning. Needless to say, she quickly revised her vocabulary.

So would you like to try the exercise yourself? How many ways can you say the "M" word? Take three minutes to jot down your slang terms. What if you had to stand up in front of a class of your peers and read the list aloud? Would you experience any shame?

I ask because shame is one of the most destructive tools in Satan's arsenal. Some cynics say there'd be no shame if masturbation were morally right. Shame wouldn't exist if the individual weren't, in reality, guilty. But they forget that shame is typically passed from generation to generation. Parents become embarrassed when their little children innocently touch themselves in public: "Don't do that; it's not right!" Such messages, coupled with the silence, create shame when adolescent sexual urges kick in at full throttle.

This baggage has been handed down over the centuries. During the Victorian era, sexual acts just weren't discussed. Sex was only for procreation, and to ask a married man or woman if they engaged in intercourse was shamefully revealing. Since that time, we've been able to have healthier conversations about sexuality. We are allowed to talk about sex in the context of marriage as being a natural and normal part of life. It no longer has to be hidden or ignored. This openness has helped to dispel some of the shame.

WILL YOU LET YOUR BIBLICAL WISDOM SHINE?

While Scripture speaks to almost every other sexual issue, it's silent on masturbation. So what do we do now? We make it a matter of wise choice. When Scripture is silent, we apply wisdom by looking at correlating issues where Scripture speaks clearly. That means masturbation will fall into the same category as, for example, the question about eating meat sacrificed to idols (something that bothered lots of early Christians). Take a "time-out" now to read and meditate on the apostle Paul's words about this:

> *Accept him whose faith is weak, without passing judgment on disputable matters. One man's faith allows him to eat everything, but another man, whose faith is weak, eats only vegetables. The man who eats everything must not look down on him who does not, and the man who does not eat everything must not condemn the man who does, for God has accepted him. . . .*
>
> *If we live, we live to the Lord; and if we die, we die to the Lord. So, whether we live or die, we belong to the Lord.*
>
> *For this very reason, Christ died and returned to life so that he might be the Lord of both the dead and the living. You, then, why do you judge your brother? Or why do you look down on your brother? For we will all stand before God's judgment seat. . . .*
>
> *As one who is in the Lord Jesus, I am fully convinced that no food is unclean in itself. But if anyone regards something as unclean, then for him it is unclean. . . .*
>
> *Let us therefore make every effort to do what leads to peace and to mutual edification. Do not destroy the work of God for the sake of food. All food is clean, but it is wrong for a man to eat anything that causes someone else to stumble. It is better not to eat meat or drink wine or to do anything else that will cause your brother to fall.*
>
> *So whatever you believe about these things keep between yourself and God. Blessed is the man who does not condemn himself by what he approves. But the man who has doubts is*

condemned if he eats, because his eating is not from faith; and
everything that does not come from faith is sin. (Romans 14:1-3,
8-10,14,19-23)

Can you see a similarity in the nature of "gray" issues, things about which believers might agree or disagree? With all such questions, we need to discern the proper balance between liberty and restriction. We do it by taking a solid look at Scripture and sincerely inviting the Holy Spirit to give us insight and guidance. Then we formulate a personal view. This is how it worked for two guys I know, whom I'll call Jason and Justin.

Jason firmly concludes, "No way this is right." For some of you it will become evident that masturbation is sin. After reading this book you may come to the solid conclusion that masturbation isn't something you can engage in without it compromising your relationship with God.

That's how it was for Jason. He was raised to believe that masturbation was a *universal* sin that kept *all* men, including himself, from experiencing the blessings of God. He couldn't biblically support his view directly, but he believed it to be true based on the strong sense of guilt he would experience.

In fact, he firmly believed that masturbation had control over him and that the same was true of all men. He believed that the difference between him and other guys was that he was being honest about this sin while others were in denial.

"I never talked about it, but my dad talked about it, and I just listened. My dad just said it was a bad habit — not that it's wrong, but that I shouldn't let it control me."   **—Rick, 16**

We met weekly and began to pray and explore what Scripture says about everything from sexuality to his sense of immobilizing guilt. After some time, Jason concluded that masturbation wasn't as universal a sin issue as he thought. He also realized that his judgment of others was an attempt to make himself feel better about his own guilt. He began to view masturbation as a gray issue rather than as purely black or white.

As we talked, he told me that for the first time, he had a strong sense of peace about this issue because he was now more biblically and culturally informed. He also recognized some of the cultural ideas that had been passed on from past eras. These ideas were built on misconceptions and false notions. He sensed a new freedom for himself. When I asked him what his personal view of masturbation was he said, "I am convinced that there is freedom for some in this issue, but for me, it's a sin." This young man felt the bondage of doubt, guilt, judgment, and shame being lifted. He can now see this as sin in his life yet not stand condemned.

> *When we masturbate, some of us come to our Father and say, "I've masturbated again, and I'm not worthy to be called your son." He brushes that aside, saying, "No one but Jesus is worthy to be called my Son, but I love you and forgive you." He demonstrates that love by presenting us with a ring, robe, and shoes. Then He says, "In case you forgot, Jesus picked these up at Calvary for you. That makes you worthy enough for me. Now let's celebrate and enjoy each other!"*[1]

Jason was able to identify what part of the issue was sin and where it was rooted for him. He also found a new freedom in allowing God to step into his life in a new and healing way. For him, the immobilizing shame and guilt that had always formed a dooming cloud over him was replaced by a personal conviction that motivated him to run to God and find acceptance.

Justin simply affirms, "Hey, I've always been free in Christ!" After reading this book you may conclude you have complete freedom with mastur-bation; it isn't a sin for you, while some may find masturbation to be matters of personal sin. Like Justin, you will discover freedom in Christ.

Yet remember: Gray issues that allow liberty in the Christian life still come packaged with guidelines. Being informed about an issue and understanding it—as well as the guidelines surrounding it—require prayerful wisdom.

We'll delve into specific guidelines later in this book. But for now, remember the pastor I spoke about in the Introduction? After we prayed together, he said to me, "I have a fourteen-year-old son. I've never talked to him about masturbation because of my own shame and guilt and because I've never been able to resolve the issue in my own mind. Now I can't wait to get home and help my son discern if there may be freedom for him."

After reading this book you may come to a similar personal con-clusion—that masturbation is a wisdom issue and that it can be engaged in under certain guidelines of Christian liberty as Justin did. Others will come to the conclusion that masturbation is a wisdom issue in which, while all things are lawful, not all things are wise (see 1 Corinthians 6:12), making it a personal sin issue as Jason did. It is my prayer that all will come into a new freedom, having the ability to for-mulate a biblically and culturally informed personal view.

After all, why should we allow Satan to keep us in a state of immobility, false guilt, and shame? The apostle Paul tells us in

Galatians 5 that it was for freedom that Jesus saved us. And we shall be free indeed!

In the next chapter we'll take a quick walk through history to see how Christians of the past have dealt with masturbation. We don't live in a vacuum. Those who have gone before us have prepared the way for our thinking today.

THINK ABOUT IT!

1. Do you agree that the issue of masturbation is a "silent struggle" for most Christian guys? Why, or why not?

2. Think about a time when you were most aware of the silence. How did it affect you? What was the role of guilt? Fear? Shame?

3. Which of the "fear factors" most directly applies to your own experience? How do you think the author might counsel a guy who's struggling with this particular fear?

4. With which of the guys do you most closely identify—Jason or Justin? Why?

5. What do you hope to gain by reading this book? (Suggestion: Make a brief list of your most pressing questions; jot new insights and information as you read.)

CHAPTER TWO

THE *REAL* BIG M: MONSTERS AND MYTHS FROM HISTORY

> *In my opinion, neither the plague, nor war, nor the pox, nor a host of similar evils, have more disastrous results for humanity than this fatal habit.* —DR. REVEILLE-PARISE, 1828

On a wintry day in 1890—or 1950—you walk into the doctor's office suffering from a common cold. You describe some of your symptoms, but after a few moments the doctor interrupts, "Son, you need to be completely honest with me."

He then confronts you to see if you ever touch yourself, even when you shower. You admit that you touch yourself; you can't wash without touching yourself.

He notices that you have a little acne or that your walk is "different" or that your appetite seems abnormal. So you start to feel shame under his probing, and you can't look him in the eye. He becomes more convinced that he's on the right track, because he knows one of the symptoms is bashfulness.

"How much do you touch yourself, and for how long have you been doing this?"

"I'm not exactly sure," you stammer. Because you appear to be confused, he's convinced you're losing your mental capacity. He points these things out to you, so you correct him. You boldly state that you are offended by his accusations of immorality, and you tell him. The doctor recognizes two more signs: your apparent impudence and a false piety. He's convinced you're suffering from a secret, solitary affliction.

As if that weren't bad enough, the doctor and your pastor eventually confront your parents, who should have been decent enough to recognize the warning signs. Now your parents are equally ashamed.

And you sit in your room wondering, day after day, *How will I ever live this down?*

SURVEYING THE HISTORICAL HYSTERIA

Beginning in the 1950s, the medical community would begin admitting some mistakes. Nevertheless, many of the misconceptions advanced in earlier eras still survive in some form today. (We'll look at four of the big ones in the next chapter.) It seems that each new generation continues to hand down its fears, shames, and myths to the next.

So how, exactly, did we arrive where we are today? Clearly, our views about masturbation didn't just spring up over night. In fact, Satan has attached shame to this issue down through the centuries. He's used powerful, articulate (and well-meaning) men to serve as so-called experts, propagating myriad myths and misconceptions.

Are you ready to take a closer look at this unfolding story? Let's take a whirlwind ride through history, briefly touching down within some key eras. We'll discover several famous personalities whose medical and/or theological ideas continue to shape our thinking today.

The 400s B.C. — *Dr. Hippocrates proclaims a "no touch" approach to conservation.*

To trace the historical context of masturbation we have to start with the Father of Medicine, Hippocrates. This man held to the belief, long popular within ancient civilizations, that semen and vaginal fluids contained life-giving powers and were therefore vital for health. From this belief came the *semen-conservation theory.*

The basic premise? That the loss or discharge of semen weakened a man and made him susceptible to disease and death. The more a man engaged in sexual activity to the point of arousal or orgasm, the more he jeopardized his life expectancy — a high price to pay for a moment of pleasure! Every discharge, whether it occurred at arousal or was the result of a nocturnal emission (wet dream) or came from orgasm during intercourse, shortened a man's life.

The preventive response seemed obvious: Engage in as little sexual activity as possible. Because some forms of seminal and vaginal discharge cannot be controlled, it became important to at least control as much as possible. So Hippocrates would say that sex for pleasure was a gross overindulgence. If a guy wanted to conserve his life-giving fluids, then he'd need to save them for the purpose of procreation only. After all, why not minimize health risks if you can?

"I thought I only had a certain amount of sperm — if I masturbated a lot, then I would run out. So I tried not to do it."
— Paul, 19

Hippocrates even identified a masturbatory disorder that affects the "spinal marrow," leading to symptoms of fever, twitching, consumption, headaches, ringing in the ears, loss of breath, weakness, and infertility. This disorder, according to Hippocrates, arose from the loss of great quantities of seminal fluid.[1] This disorder would be studied and expounded more thoroughly by the medical minds of the Victorian era.

The Late 300s A.D. — Reverend Augustine concludes: "Spirit good, fire bad" (avoid those flames of passion).

This great bishop of Hippo, in Africa, became awesomely influential in the history of the church. His accomplishments for the kingdom of God are well known.

However, Saint Augustine did have a questionable viewpoint about sex. In fact, he believed that anything sexual was pure evil. Adam and Eve were expelled from the Garden of Eden because of sexual intercourse, among other things. Sexual thoughts, desires, drives, and behavior — even in marriage — were considered wicked. Augustine still had to contend with God's command to "be fruitful and multiply" (Genesis 9:1, NASB). Therefore, intercourse became a necessity, but only for producing children.

Why would this bishop espouse such extreme views? Perhaps it had to do with his youthful struggles with lust, especially before he converted to Christianity:

> From the time of his first visit to the great city of Carthage, when he was about sixteen, Augustine seldom lost an opportunity to pursue one sin or another; or so he tells us in his Confessions. He took a mistress when he was seventeen or eighteen and fathered an illegitimate son before he was twenty. About that same time, he began a relationship with a religious and philosophical system known as Manichaeism, which claimed that two

principles, Light and Dark, God and Matter, are eternal. . . .

[But] one by one, Augustine found that his assorted intel-
lectual, moral, and spiritual objections to Christianity had been
stripped away. In 386, in a villa outside of Rome, he underwent
one of the more dramatic conversions in the history of the
Christian church. After hearing a voice say, "Take up and read,"
Augustine recounts that he picked up "the volume of the Apostle."

"I seized it and opened it, and in silence I read the first pas-
sage on which my eyes fell. 'No orgies or drunkenness, no
immorality or indecency . . . stop giving attention to your sin-
ful nature, to satisfy its desires.'"[2]

Augustine's pre-conversion experience with unbounded sexuality
must have made him ashamed of his past and determined to help other
young people avoid his mistakes. And his early flirtations with
Manichean philosophy may also have tainted some of his later views
with Gnostic thought—something Paul had warned the early church
about (in the Book of Colossians, for instance).

You see, the Gnostics believed there was a separation of matter and
spirit. God operated in the spirit, thus making spirit pure and good.
Physical material, on the other hand, was inherently evil. This meant
that the body was wicked. Anything required to sustain the body—
like eating, drinking, breathing—while essential, was evil as well.
Therefore the ultimate evil would be to indulge the body.

You guessed it: Sex for pleasure became a wicked no-no.

**The 1200s—*Professor Thomas Aquinas thinks it's all about
thinking. Aquinas was one of the church's greatest
thinkers, teachers, and writers.***

He applied his scholarly mind to all kinds of theological questions, even coming up with some powerful proofs for the existence of God.

So it's not surprising that Aquinas also tried sorting out the question of sexuality and spirituality. Like most of his theological ancestors, he still held that intercourse was for baby-making only. His unique spin, though, was that the *intent* of intercourse was for procreation. If married people engaged in sex with the *intent* in their hearts to produce a child—if the motive was to make babies only—then the act itself wasn't evil or shameful. Think right, do right. For Thomas, this better harmonized with God's command to multiply. Still, any sexual act that didn't lead to procreation was considered sinful.

This also led Aquinas to define *natural* and *unnatural* sexual acts.[3] Unnatural sexual acts didn't produce offspring, so masturbation was therefore an unnatural act. Aquinas believed masturbation was among the greatest of sexual sins. He said that sex with prostitutes was actually less sinful because fornication was far more natural than masturbation and therefore the lesser of evils. Incest wasn't as wicked as masturbation because it could result in procreation, which was natural!

One note here: It's hard to tell when the word *masturbation* first arose in history. The word could have been compounded from the Latin *manus*, meaning "hand," and *sturpore*, meaning "to defile." Thus the act is an unnatural defilement with one's hand. Later, in the Victorian era, the word would be replaced entirely, and the act would be known as "self-abuse," hinting that the Victorians held to this derivative of the word.

Others scholars traced the word to the Latin *manus* coupled with *tubare*, meaning "to disturb."[4] This is a less condemning view, seeing the act as simply a disturbance, or stimulation, by hand. Other scholars concur with a less condemning meaning, citing the Greek compound of *mazdo*, a "virile member," and *turbu*, also meaning "to disturb."[5] Aquinas would have held to the earlier derivative of the Latin context of the word.

The 1500s — *The Reformers allow a little pleasure — but watch out for the demons!*

During the era of the Protestant Reformation, the Reformers held to a broader view of sexual arousal and intercourse. They began letting go of some unnecessary baggage, especially the idea of not allowing sex to be pleasurable. In addition, prior to the Reformation, the clergy (or anyone who was set apart for the service of God) were required to remain celibate. Remaining pure and holy had meant no sex, not even for procreation. But many of the Reformers believed clergy could and should marry. And procreation wasn't the only thing they had on their minds.

Yet the semen-conservation view prevailed, and masturbation was still "unnatural" and therefore evil. It was considered a form of "self-pollution," ultimately poisoning a person both physically and morally, thus making it a "mortal sin"[6] Many theologians through the centuries, including some Reformers, also believed that masturbation was provoked by demons, who would seduce men to do it. These demons would collect the semen from masturbation and wet dreams and use it to generate bodies they could inhabit. Or they would use it to impregnate women, producing demonic offspring.[7]

The proof of this demon-baby theory? Birth defects!

The Early 1700s — *An anonymous writer sparks medical paranoia and moral panic.*

In the early 1700s masturbation was commonly termed *onanism*. The term comes from the Old Testament personality Onan. He was thought to be judged by God because "he spilled his semen on the ground" (Genesis 38:9), which was a sin punishable by death. (We'll dig deeply into this passage in chapter 5.)

In 1715 an anonymous writer published an intriguing essay in London. Here is its title:

Onania: The heinous sin of self-pollution and all its
frightful consequences, in both sexes considered, with spiritual
and physical advice to those who have already injured
themselves by this abominable practice; and seasonable
admonition to the Youth of the Nation (of both sexes) and
those whose tuition they are under, whether parents,
guardians, masters, or mistresses.

I guess the title says it all. Hundreds of thousands of copies of this essay spread throughout England and Europe like wildfire, undergoing many revisions and additions by yet many more anonymous authors. It was widely accepted and endorsed by the medical and religious community. Its basic premise was that grave physical consequences came from masturbating because this practice was rooted in the vilest of all sins against nature. The ultimate fate of the masturbator was death and hell. The proof of the moral consequence was connected to the physical toll that masturbation supposedly took on the masturbator. *Onania* states: "Many young men, who were strong and lusty before they gave themselves over to this vice, have been worn out by it, and by its robbing the body of its balmy and vital moisture, without coughing or spitting, dry and emaciated, sent to their graves."[8]

The Mid-1700s — *Dr. Samuel Tissot suggests, "Apply the palm, deny the brain."*

In the mid-1700s, a physician named Samuel Tissot believed the premise of *Onania,* but he was convinced that much of it wasn't written by a physician. So Tissot decided to write a medical primer titled *Onanism: A Treatise Upon the Disorders Produced by Masturbation.*

Tissot's work, catapulted by London's original anonymous essay, became the most influential work shaping the medical and religious communities' views on masturbation for two centuries to come. *Onanism* became a legitimate, scientifically acceptable treatment of the issue, even though built upon the limited medical knowledge of the times — as well as much speculation, misguided conclusions, and dogmatic opinions. It flew off the presses in many languages, though. And it was cited in countless medical journals, reference materials, case studies, and scholarly texts.

Before writing his text on masturbation, Tissot had achieved fame as a leading physician for his pioneering work with various vaccines. He became a medical advisor to the rich and famous. People flocked to his hometown of Lausanne, Switzerland, to see the great doctor. Kings offered him medical commissions as their private physician. Universities sought him to oversee their medical schools. Even the Vatican utilized his expertise. In other words, Tissot was unquestionably famous as a medical expert and scientific researcher, second to none. My point is that all of this renown meant Tissot could make medical claims and offer moral opinions that could hardly be challenged.

What were some of his claims? For one thing, based on the semen-conservation theory, he held that the loss of a single ounce of seminal fluid was equivalent to losing forty ounces of blood.[9] That meant a habitual masturbator was flirting with instant death, not to mention the countless other diseases and disorders that might precede his death. Just about any and every disease could be traced back to masturbation. Tissot proclaimed that "this deadly habit kills more youth than all diseases combined."[10]

This great medical authority also scientifically deduced that insanity and mental illness were directly connected to masturbation. Why? Because of what he observed in insane asylums. He noticed that the single most common behavior practiced by the patients—outside of eating, sleeping, and defecating—was masturbating. It was Tissot's opinion that the loss of seminal and vaginal fluids was killing these patients.

Tissot also discovered, through deductive reasoning, another danger factor. When a person becomes aroused, the soft, erectile tissue of the penis or clitoris engorges with blood. This process is called vasocongestion (for guys it's more commonly known as an erection). Tissot deduced that the vasocongestion of the genitals deprived other organs, particularly the brain, of proper blood flow. And organ tissue deprived of blood would become weak and diseased, right? So, we now have excessive masturbation keeping blood from the brain, thereby killing off its cells. This, Tissot surmised, ultimately led to insanity.[11]

In addition, sexual thinking excited the nervous system, putting excess strain on it. The nervous system could take this strain occasionally when intercourse was necessary for reproduction. But masturbation was an abuse of the system. Can you imagine what Tissot's public service commercial would sound like on television today? How about something like this:

> # THIS IS YOUR BRAIN.
> ## THIS IS YOUR BRAIN FROM MASTURBATING.
> ## TOUCHING YOURSELF CAN KILL YOU.
> ## ANY QUESTIONS?

It wasn't long before the medical community began to claim that any loss of function related to the brain (such as senses) was caused by masturbation. If a teen's eyesight started to fail, it was probably due to excessive masturbation damaging the sight-controlling area of his brain. (Incidentally, the blindness myth still gets some attention. A friend of mine was addressing a youth group on sexuality, and she jokingly stated, "If you masturbate, you'll go blind!" Suddenly one of the guys in the room started yelling, "I can't see, I can't see!" While this is humorous, the origins of this myth were rooted in perceived truths propagated by respected medical and religious professionals like Tissot.)

"I used to think that you could get a sexually transmitted disease from masturbating." —Lisa, 17

After making such brain connections, though without empirical proof, Tissot went on to link numerous diseases to the curse of "self-pollution." One of his famous case studies involved a seventeen-year-old boy. Tissot claimed that this young man was healthy until he began to masturbate at least once a day:

> *Not a year had elapsed before he began to feel a great weakness*
> *after every act: this notification was not sufficient to rescue him*

from his filthy practices; his soul, already devoted to these ordures,
was incapable of forming any other idea, and the repetition of his
crime became everyday more frequent, till such time as he was in a
state which gave reason to apprehend his death. Too late grown
wise, the evil had made so great a progress, that he was incurable.[12]

The doctor then describes the boy as bedridden and wasted away
to the point that he looked like an emaciated cadaver. Here's his
description upon arriving at the boy's home:

What I found was less a living being than a cadaver lying
on straw, thin, pale, exuding a loathsome stench, almost
incapable of movement. A pale and watery blood often
dripped from his nose; he drooled continually: subject to
attacks of diarrhea, he defecated in his bed without noticing
it; there was a constant flow of semen; his eyes, sticky,
blurry, dull, had lost all power of movement; his pulse was
extremely weak and racing; labored respiration, extreme emaci-
ation, except for the feet, which were showing signs of edema.
Mental disorder was equally evident; without ideas, without
memory, incapable of linking two sentences, without reflec-
tion, without fear of his fate, lacking all feeling except that of
pain, which returned at least every three days with each new
attack. Thus sunk below the level of the beast, a spectacle of
unimaginable horror, it was difficult to believe that he had
once belonged to the human race.[13]

A few weeks later, this unfortunate boy died. He had masturbated
himself to death. So . . . if the good doctor is to be believed, then:
Gentlemen, it is time to stop masturbating!

The Early 1800s — *Reverend Sylvester Graham creates an amazing, lust-fighting diet.*

In the early 1800s a preacher named Sylvester Graham appeared on the scene. Becoming a popular itinerant preacher, he was articulate and charismatic as a speaker, able to hold the attention of a crowd for hours. At first he focused on the evils of alcohol during the temperance movement. But eventually he shifted to the evils of masturbation.

Actually, Graham believed alcoholism was one the results of masturbation, and his hellfire-and-brimstone tactics produced a shameful guilt. His listeners who had experienced masturbation would slink away under a cloud of shame. Parents would also know the same shame and guilt when they didn't raise their children on the disciplined Grahamite diet and exercise that was needed to keep them pure. You see, the cure, according to Graham, came from avoiding sinful indulgences and was disciplined by a rigid diet and a routine exercise program. Certain foods and drinks could produce unclean, polluting desires that could awaken demonic sexual lusts. How easily these lusts overtake a person!

Of course, Graham had a lock on which foods were good and bad. For example, he believed that meat was absolutely forbidden, basing the idea on the fact that *carne*, or meat, produced the "carnal" qualities of fleshly sin. To Graham and his followers, it was so obvious that the apostle Paul's writing on carnality was linked to meat. Therefore, Graham promoted vegetarianism as a deterrent to fleshly lust. He didn't stop with the elimination of meat from one's diet, though. He believed that spices, especially salts, not only excited taste but also excited lustful passions.[14]

Graham didn't realize that sex hormones, responsible for normal sexual development and growth, also stimulated sexual thought.

Instead, he believed that certain foods produced these lusts and should be eliminated. He also thought certain foods should be eaten to *prevent* lusts. That's why he started to produce a ground meal made up of certain grains he'd seen his mother use in the baking of bread. This recipe, according to Graham, would purify the system. His food, the Graham Cracker, became an anti-masturbatory food. (Today we know Graham for his cracker but not for the horror that preceded it. I told a friend this story, and he commented jokingly that maybe youth pastors always serve s'mores at retreats because they subconsciously—or divinely— know that the Graham Cracker will keep students sexually pure.)

These misconceptions of Tissot's and Graham's would become the start of a great medical crusade built on the premise that the *secret sin of masturbation* was an epidemic ripe for exposure. Some of the most abusive practices and gross misconceptions ever advanced by the medical and religious communities soon followed. Welcome to the Victorian era.

The Late 1800s — *Nice Victorians see sex as . . . sick, sick, sick!*

At the turn of the nineteenth century and into the early twentieth century masturbation was marked as being self-polluting, self-abusing, and the most "heinous sin" one could commit. Much of the literature from the Victorian era describes it as the most heinous sin. It was in face a form of suicide to them. With this sin came grave physical and moral consequences. Naturally, a kind of moral panic set in. It has been said that this "whole era might well be called the age of masturbatory insanity."[15]

Sexuality surely wasn't to be enjoyed. Obviously, if a person could jeopardize his or her life by becoming frequently aroused, then anything that led to sexual arousal should be avoided. The Victorian era was so prudish that women viewed themselves as nonsexual beings. They supposedly had no sexual desires, sexual thoughts, or sexual feelings.

Male sexuality was viewed as a part of masculine virility—necessary for procreation, but not to be overindulged. While sex for pleasure was unspeakable, it was an acceptable double standard for a man to be a sexual being, but not for a woman. A real man could sire children, but he would never talk about sex as being fun (or say that he even engaged in it). One could never admit to feeling or thinking sexually, out of fear of becoming aroused or being labeled a pervert.

If sexual pleasure was immoral, then the ultimate immorality was masturbation. What a terrible crime it was! Forbidden by God, and so filthy that it was shameful for decent people to talk about. This shameful silence thrived upon the way doctors, teachers, and clergy addressed sexual issues in general. A medical dictionary of the day stated that masturbation was "a vice not decent to name, but productive of the most deplorable and generally incurable disorders." That same dictionary went on to say that it is "a crime not to be mentioned, much less to be practiced, in a country where virtue, decency or politeness have the least regard paid to them."[16]

This era set the stage for much of the misconceptions, fears, shame, and silence that plague the issue today. In fact, the Victorian era became the "high-water mark of anxiety over masturbation. . . . Scaremongering about the habit did more harm than the habit itself."[17] Many of the medical texts and dictionaries of this era concurred with Tissot that masturbation led to disease, mental incompetence, and ultimately death.[18] So long is the list of symptoms and sicknesses attributed to masturbation, that I've included appendix A at the back of this book just to list a few of the major ones. (Take a break from your reading and turn there now, if you like. Noticed any of these symptoms in yourself lately?)

From that list, you could deduce that masturbation was at the root of every health issue. If you stop to think about it, that puts the doctor in a position of power and infallibility. If he didn't know what to do or how to diagnose a disorder, then he could just play the masturbation card. If the patient never admitted to masturbating and would not be cured, then the doctor was right and the person's wicked vice consumed him or her. If the person did admit to masturbating and was not cured, then the doctor could emphatically state that the masturbation was so chronic that the person became incurable.

Doctors urged their patients to confess to masturbating in order to save their lives from disease and their souls from hell.[19] Medical doctors believed that this practice provoked the judgment of God. It was therefore their moral obligation to confront the "sin" and not just treat the symptoms. In addition, the medical and religious community challenged parents, teachers, and guardians to beware the grave consequences of masturbation and take preventive measures.

But here's the problem: The average, normal development of an adolescent includes growing pains, muscle spasms resulting from rapid bone growth, acne, changes in sleep patterns, and so on. But it seems that no matter what ailed a young person, it was traced back to masturbation. Because most adolescent guys and many adolescent women do masturbate, a doctor would diagnose the teen as suffering the consequences of this deadly, wicked vice. And eight out of ten times in males and four out of ten times in females, that diagnosis would ring shamefully true.

Remember the semen-conservation theory? Well, the Victorian medical community confused the bodily effects of sex hormones with that of semen and vaginal fluids. They believed semen and vaginal secretions were responsible for puberty. If a child learned the habit of masturbation, then he or she wouldn't develop at a normal rate. A person who was late in his or her physical development was therefore exposed as a masturbator. Women were exposed by their lack of maturity, often seen in their giddiness and sensitive emotions.

It was easier to detect in men, who were naturally more at risk of masturbation because the loss of semen was a far greater physical problem than the loss of vaginal fluid. Men who seemed "less manly" were showing the early signs of their secret sin. It would become a common belief that masturbation robbed men of their masculinity. Thus puberty and the physical development of adolescence produced a "no win" situation for teens. Either you were a masturbator because you showed the signs of normal development, or you were a masturbator because you *didn't!*

Eventually, doctors declared masturbation to be the number-one killer of adolescents. One prominent doctor of the era said, "This abominable practice has put to death more individuals than all the great wars, joined to the most depopulating epidemics."[20] Another influential medical professor, in his book titled *Satan in Society,* described masturbation as a shameful and criminal act, being the most fatal of all vices.[21] (Of course the book title itself pretty much gives away his bias, right?)

Another medical text stated, "Masturbation is one of those scourges which secretly attack and destroy humanity."[22] This text continues to say, "In my opinion, neither the plague, nor war, nor the pox, nor a host of similar evils, have more disastrous results for humanity than this fatal habit."[23] Don't forget that Dr. Tissot taught and believed that this habit killed more youth than all diseases combined.

The Early 1900s — *Dr. John Harvey Kellogg invents the ultimate cure: cold showers and cornflakes.*

Another famous person jumped on the anti-masturbatory-food bandwagon. That man was a medical doctor named John Harvey Kellogg. In the early 1900s, Kellogg produced the Cornflake as an anti-masturbatory food. Dr. Kellogg concurred with Graham about dietary issues, but he took things a step further.

Kellogg grew up under the teachings of the Seventh-Day Adventist founding leader, Ellen White, and became the appointed medical superintendent of the Western Health Reformed Institute, founded by Mrs. White. This allowed Dr. Kellogg an opportunity to practice various forms of treatments for all types of diseases. Like Graham, he propagated doctrines on sexual abstinence, dietary revisions, and exercise. Many of these doctrines are still held to be true by Adventists today.[24] He also combined the work and beliefs of James Jackson into his belief system.

Jackson believed personal hygiene was essential to purity. After all, the external parts should not be kept *un*clean! He pioneered hydropathic therapies, or water cures. He believed that people should soak for long periods of time, take cold showers, and apply hot and cold wet-packs to the genitalia. (Today, some people still believe the myth that cold showers eliminate or control sexual desire and arousal.)

Kellogg incorporated these cold showers and soaking into his therapies. He even believed that various types of enemas should be administered daily to cleanse the system of any impurities. He also practiced many of these preventive measures himself.

"I used to believe that if you had too many erections from masturbating, then you'd become impotent when you got married."
—Ben, 17

Kellogg ultimately became the director of the Battle Creek Sanitarium, a center for the learning and practice of preventive health and purity. Kellogg's ideas and fame spread far and wide. People would flock to his sanitarium for teaching and treatment. Today we still have the Cornflake, although we don't use it as an anti-masturbatory food. However, some folks still hold too many of Kellogg's quacky views.

Kellogg devised a series of thirty-seven warning signs that physicians could look for to uncover whether a young patient was a masturbator:[25]

1. general debility
2. consumption-like symptoms
3. premature and defective development
4. sudden changes in disposition
5. lassitude (fatigue)
6. sleeplessness
7. failure of mental capacity
8. fickleness
9. untrustworthiness
10. love of solitude
11. bashfulness
12. unnatural boldness
13. mock piety
14. being easily frightened
15. confusion of ideas
16. aversion to girls in boys, but a liking for boys in girls
17. round shoulders
18. weak backs and stiffness of joints
19. paralysis of the lower extremities
20. unnatural gait
21. bad position in bed

22. lack of breast development in females

23. capricious appetite

24. fondness for unnatural, hurtful, or irritating articles

25. disgust at simple foods

26. use of tobacco

27. unnatural paleness

28. acne or pimples

29. biting of fingernails

30. shifty eyes

31. moist, cold hands

32. palpitations of the heart

33. hysteria in females

34. chlorosis, or the green sickness

35. epileptic fits

36. bed-wetting

37. the use of obscene words and phrases

Obviously, just about every person ever born exhibits some of these symptoms during a lifetime. Such a list gives you the flavor of the hysteria created by men like Kellogg. They were literally on a witch-hunt. Nobody was exempt—except those with medical authority. They were detached from such wickedness and spoke condescendingly about the issue. Their countless case studies were rarely verified, usually based on secondhand or embellished stories. What else but false guilt, debilitating shame, and a fearful silence can flow from such abusive tactics?

(Let's take a breather right here. You might turn to Appendix B for a moment, where you'll find descriptions of some of the extreme "preventive measures" that were once used to keep young people from masturbating. Some of the preventions and cures, like the nutritional changes to diet, were mild. Other measures were—obviously!—much more severe.)

THE MYTHS KEEP GOING, AND GOING, AND . . .

Many people still believe various forms of the previous myths and misconceptions, and thus these ideas have stayed with us after haunting us for centuries. Even as late as the 1950s, some physicians believed that masturbation caused disease. Many in that decade also believed that masturbation caused stupidity, mental illness, and insanity.[26] I have spoken with students who believe masturbation has affected their energy levels, making them more susceptible to sickness (which, of course, they believed was a punishment sent by God). Some students believed only homosexuals would masturbate—or that if you did masturbate, then you'd *become* a homosexual. When I pressed one student about this, he concluded, "If you like touching a penis so much, then you *must* be gay."

In 1934, after undergoing fifty-seven printings and selling almost five million copies, *The Handbook for Boys* (published by The Boy Scouts of America) still adhered to a semen-conservation theory. The book states,

> *Any habit which a boy has that causes this fluid to be discharged from the body tends to weaken his strength, to make him less able to resist disease, and often unfortunately fastens upon him habits which later in life can be broken only with great difficulty. Even several years before this fluid appears in the body such habits are harmful to a growing boy.*[27]

Of course, the habit, which is never stated outright, is masturbation. These myths continued to appear in literature throughout the twentieth century and into the twenty-first century.

Whew! Have you ever taken such a quick trip through twenty-five centuries? I hope it wasn't too painful for you. And I hope it gave you some encouragement, seeing that we've made at least some progress in our attitudes.

Over the years it would begin to come out that the medical community made some mistakes. Wow, what a relief — or is it? The religious community held to the same truth and harmonized them with doctrine. Successive generations pass down their fears, shame, and misconceptions to the next without questioning.

We must remember that Satan is responsible for two distinct activities: He tempts us to sin and then he accuses us of our sin. The first we understand because we know how he takes evil things and makes them look very attractive. We tend to forget the second. He accuses to immobilize, defeat, and destroy believers. He takes good things, such as moral consensus, medicine, and even Scripture, and twists them out of context. I am not saying that masturbation is good, nor am I saying that it is bad. If we are to formulate an informed personal view of masturbation, we must realize that much of the residual of the past is built on lies. Moral, ethical, and supposedly God-honoring ideas were founded on error. This bred a hateful, condemning, and judgmental vocal authority who derived their information from pagan and Gnostic roots about semen conservation, dietary needs, and the evil of flesh. They formulated abusive practices, publicly shamed people, and openly exposed anything in opposition to them as heretical. It was no different from The Inquisition or the witch-hunts of earlier days. This doesn't make masturbation right, but seeing the foundational lies allows us to level the playing field to formulate a personal view.

So are you ready to dig in to the next topic? In chapter 3 we'll be looking at how certain historical misconceptions have shaped and sustained the *modern* myths that still linger today.

THINK ABOUT IT!

1. Which of the historical myths were most surprising to you? Which beliefs seemed the most bizarre?

2. In what ways have you seen the influence of historical misconception still affecting young people in your own generation?

3 If you could change one attitude about masturbation that you find in the church today, what would it be? Why?

4. In your opinion, what role has fear played in the history of anti-masturbation misinformation? What fears still exist in our day?

5. How would you distinguish between a healthy shame and an unhealthy shame when it comes to sexuality? Where are you, personally, in terms of shame, sexuality, and spirituality?

CHAPTER THREE

CONFRONT THESE MODERN-DAY MYTHS!

*I've prayed and asked God to help me, but I think I've gone too
far. I think I need rehab.*

The hunter rose early to get to his favorite blind and await a choice
duck. Hour after hour he waited, but no flying prey. Then, just as he'd
decided to call it a day . . . *Quack, quack!*

He looked into the distance, and sitting there on the water, per-
fectly still, was a beautiful mallard. The hunter raised his gun and fired,
splintering his long-awaited dinner into a thousand pieces.

Another hunter's head popped up from some nearby bushes. With
duck horn falling from his lips, he shouted, "Hey, why did you kill my
decoy?" The moral of the story: *If it looks like a duck and quacks like a duck,
it may* not *be a duck.*

Some say masturbation is an outright sin because it looks and feels
like sin. But remember that Satan is a master of deception, specializing
in decoys. Often the support for an ironclad "universal sin theory" is
rooted in modern-day myths. A claim may come from a leader whose
authority won't be challenged. A claim may *sound* true (it quacks like a
duck). A claim may *appear* to be valid (it looks like a duck). But when
probed and exposed, suppose a statement can't be validated? Is it really
a duck after all?

Let's look more closely at some of the modern-day claims about masturbation. We might call them the "Big Four M-Myths" of today.

THE ADDICTION MYTH: "YOU'RE A DIRTY, ROTTEN SEX JUNKIE, MY BOY!"

Kevin was a seventeen-year-old high school junior in the youth group where I was a youth pastor. He met me after school one day. As we sat down together at McDonald's, he quietly leaned across the table and told me, "I need help for a very severe problem."

I'd never seen Kevin this intense or distraught before. He told me that he had a sexual addiction.

"A sexual addiction?" I asked.

"Yeah. I've been masturbating since I was twelve. I do it every day—sometimes more than once a day too. I can't stop doing it, either. I've tried, but I go about a week or two and then I can't take it anymore. I give in. I've prayed and asked God to help me, but I think I've gone too far. I think I need rehab."

Kevin had read somewhere that habitual masturbation was a sexual addiction. This is not true. Let's be clear. Addictions *do* involve habitual and repetitive behaviors, but not all habits are addictions. As a matter of fact, no sexual study has ever provided any evidence that masturbation is addictive.

Some studies have shown that masturbation cannot compare with the relational and emotional satisfaction that comes with intercourse.[1] Obviously, when people are engaging in regular intercourse, they have little need to masturbate. If masturbation was in fact addictive, then they would not be able to stop their previous behavior.

Yet I said that there is *little* proof of addiction because we must be realistic and avoid dogmatic statements giving the impression that masturbation is *never* addictive. I am sure that some study or some individual will come forward to show that masturbation can be addictive. (*Anything* can be addictive, even religion or ministry.) But the fact remains that this would be the exception, not the norm. To give the impression that regular masturbation is, or leads to, a sexual addiction is like saying that anyone who drinks is a substance abuser or potential alcoholic.

There are people who have sexual addictions. They are addicted to *sex*. A sexual addiction involves masturbation in the context of other things. That is, a sexual addiction almost never has masturbation as its exclusive behavior, but masturbation is almost always involved in the sexual behaviors of the addict. The sexual addict masturbates habitually, seeks sexual encounters habitually, views pornographic material habitually — among a host of other habitual sexual behaviors.

But lots of guys, like Kevin, do fear they are addicted. So let's take a moment to review just what we mean by the idea of "addiction." After reading the following points, I hope you'll be able to distinguish between a merely repetitive behavior and an addictive behavior.

Addictions often involve:

An unreasonable, extravagant amount of time. The addict spends virtually every waking hour obtaining, engaging in, recovering from, and hiding the addiction. For example, someone with a food addiction hoards food and is either eating food or thinking about it. His day revolves around food, which is the focal point of his life. The same is true with a sexual addiction. Masturbation becomes just one behavior in a daily plot or hunt to acquire sex.

A lifestyle pattern filled with out-of-control behaviors. The addict has a control problem in general. There may be excessive spending, for instance, to keep the addiction alive. A sex addict pays for porn, prostitutes, phone sex, and sexual paraphernalia to nurture the addiction.

A lack of fulfillment coming from the object being abused. Sex actually becomes less and less fulfilling for the sexual addict. Instead, it becomes an obsessive *need* in his mind and life. This is why masturbation is only one behavior among many with the sexual addict. The current level of sexual activity eventually becomes insufficient to satisfy, so the addict seeks greater "highs."

An impairment of daily activities. The sex addict might miss days of work, social events, and personal appointments. He may let slide such routine activities as showering, eating, or paying bills. (I have never known a guy to miss social events or appointments because of masturbation!)

A primary coping strategy in life. The addict "medicates" himself with sex. In effect, it's his drug of choice for eliminating problems, anxieties, and fears. Yes, some guys may use masturbation as a relief from stress, just as others use working out for the same purpose. However, a coping strategy means the addict resorts to the object of addiction actually to solve or ignore his problems. This doesn't work, so the addict must engage in the activity at a greater rate and with greater intensity.

A destructive force in relationships. The addict gets caught in lies. He values his addiction more than his family and friends. He abuses friends, family, coworkers, and acquaintances to protect his addiction. He doesn't follow through with the promises and normal commitments required of all relationships.

A constant display of severe mood changes. The addict becomes paranoid or enraged if he doesn't have his regular fix. He may appear elated or evasive afterward, though. And he'll likely become depressed and/or aggressive when the fix wears off.

A persistent involvement in high-risk, self-destructive behaviors. These activities serve to keep the addiction alive. The addict may gain an arrest record—maybe because he's been caught having public sex or soliciting a prostitute. He may contract sexually transmitted diseases, and may lose his job or career because of risky sexual contact or behaviors. It's tough for him to keep behavior within legal and moral boundaries.

I can guess what you're thinking at this point: *That's not me!* Well, you're probably right. Again, remember that masturbation may be an activity of a sex addict but habitual masturbation does not necessarily constitute an addiction. Not too many people miss appointments, spend gross amounts of money, suffer dramatic mood changes, lose hours in a day, and self-destruct over masturbation. Even though this may let a lot of you off the hook, this can still become a controlling issue that can lead to an addiction. Read on and see how the rest of us can develop a biblically informed, personal view on this topic.

On the other hand, they do begin to do this if they engage in pornography and sexual deviance. When masturbation accompanies these things, then there may be the beginning of an addiction. Masturbation simply becomes the reinforcer of the inappropriate sexual behavior. (That's why if you do have a true sexual addiction, you'll need to eliminate masturbation from your life.)

But wouldn't it be better never to masturbate at all? For some, this may be the road to take, given the conviction of the Holy Spirit in their life. Others may experience a broader freedom.

I observed a great example of this principle through a couple of the young men that I mentor. These two guys are incredibly buff! They both work out regularly. Dave has decided he won't eat anything unnatural for the rest of his life. He's highly disciplined and has literally eliminated sugars, soda pop, and most preservatives from his diet. He has done this for the last three years. Adam, on the other hand, is just as disciplined. But he thinks Dave is being extreme, and he often eats anything he wants.

Now, Dave could say that it's better to eliminate those foods from your life altogether so you'll be sure to avoid any adverse consequences. In reply, Adam would say that just because you *could* abuse those foods doesn't mean you will. For Dave, then, a brownie is sin. For Adam it's something to enjoy in moderation. Both approaches require clear thinking, discipline, and some obvious boundaries.

THE PSYCHO MYTH: "MY, YOU MUST BE *SO* LONELY (AND MENTALLY MESSED UP, TOO)!"

Is it true that only the lonely masturbate? This idea often surfaces in printed material and public opinion; the lonely and/or unfulfilled masturbate to compensate for their psychological problems.

I once attended a panel discussion where a leader made this claim. He stated that most men masturbate because they're attempting to fill the loneliness in their lives. I had to think that the majority of the men in the room felt like losers. Statements like this breed a devastating shame. If you hear this and you do masturbate, you would never admit to it because you would automatically be labeled a psycho freak. You could never say, "Hey, I masturbate and I'm not dealing with loneliness or any other problems right now," because masturbation seems shameful by definition.

The reverse case would also be shaming. Would anyone admit to feeling lonely if they knew they'd be looked upon with suspicion about "you know"? This is no different than what Sylvester Graham did centuries ago. He would make a statement such as "Masturbation causes disease." Anyone with a disease was humiliated, and anyone who masturbated dreaded the consequence of disease. It was a shaming, demoralizing, no-win situation no matter how you looked at it. The best recourse, then, would be to keep silent.

"I've heard it said that most guys masturbate because they can't get a partner. So if you decide not to have sex, you're a loser if you masturbate."   **—Aaron, 20**

Here's where Satan wields the same old lies with a new twist. Instead of connecting masturbation to physical issues, he couples it to a psychological issue. But loneliness, lack of fulfillment, or any other psychological problem isn't symptomatic of masturbation, or vice versa.

Is there a flip side to this coin? Yes, I certainly do know people who eat and drink out of pure boredom. There are people who use various activities to compensate, sedate, and divert their attention from their problems and personal pain. At times we all do this. Have you ever walked away from a heated conversation or gone to a movie because you couldn't handle the stress of homework? Or decided that you were going to hang out with friends because you were feeling a little depressed?

It would be foolish to say that "escape" could never be true of masturbation. Like anything else—from food to fun—masturbation can be a crutch, a diversion from reality, a form of denial, or a medication for emotional pain. The danger looms when this becomes *your sole means and strategy for coping with life*. But to say that all masturbation is a symptom of psychological problems . . . that's a myth.

THE CAUSE-AND-EFFECT MYTH: "GUESS WHAT'S CAUSING ALL YOUR TROUBLES, BRO – AND YOUR ULTIMATE DOWNFALL!"

Here we have the theory of delayed consequences: that every time something bad happens in your life, it must be the result of that secret little habit you just can't seem to give up. God is so displeased, so fed up that . . . *zap!* He sends regular, jarring lightning bolts into your days to get you to stop. Ultimately, who knows? He may have to strike you down.

Whoa! This is a serious misconception—that masturbation is a sin you'll eventually pay for and keep on paying for. I read one author who talked about one of his friends whose relationships were sabotaged because of years of masturbation. In his view, masturbation is a ticking time bomb—we never know when it's going to explode. I also read an advice column online where the counselor gave teenagers the same idea. He said that continuous masturbation will affect your future relationship with your spouse.

"I heard that if you masturbate a lot you could become a premature ejaculator because you're conditioning your body to orgasm fast." —Brian, 22

To tell you the truth, I wanted to scream, "Prove it!" What's the connection between masturbation and destroyed *future* relationships? Why aren't there countless men and many women coming forward to substantiate this claim? And are we to believe that everyone who enjoys fulfilled relationships never masturbated? Furthermore, what about the author who writes such things? I would love to ask, "Are your relationships sabotaged, or are you telling us that you never masturbated?"

Finally, other evidence actually concludes that masturbation can have positive effects on marriages.[2]

Many who make such claims, like Tissot and Graham of the past, separate themselves from the issue as if they never experienced it. It's a passive way of looking self-righteous. To see their relationships as fulfilling reinforces the deception that they never struggled with sexual desire. They are quick to point to masturbation as the "speck" in their brother's eye, but they don't notice the log in their own eye (see Matthew 7:3).

Sadly, the myth is applied not only to relationships but also to all kinds of disease. This is a bit old-fashioned today; nevertheless, you've probably heard that "it" causes blindness. What about producing hair on the knuckles? Sylvester Graham would preach up and down the New England seaboard about the physical dangers and damages of masturbation. There was nothing to substantiate his claims, but Graham and his contemporaries presented them as the absolute truth from God. Graham could direct his comments to anyone in the room and hit the mark because everyone experienced disease. He also gave the impression that he himself was never ill. He stood before his crowd as a healthy man; therefore, surely he must not be a masturbator. He never had to say that he did or didn't. All he had to do was make a bold, emphatic claim and then detach himself from the issue.

In those days, people would never question the claim of such a "great man of God." Yet today, current research has found that faulty information disseminated by "experts" can actually contribute to the development of sexual problems. In other words, the dogmatic, inaccurate information and "wisdom" proclaimed by authorities about masturbation has proven to be harmful.

THE PLEASURE MYTH: "IF IT FEELS GOOD, TOO BAD IT'S GOT TO BE WRONG . . . *RIGHT?*"

Wrong! This theory starts with the premise that masturbation is purely a selfish pleasure. And anything that is a personal pleasure obviously goes against God's will. Therefore, we must make a choice between our pleasure and God's pleasure. To choose for ourselves is sin.

It certainly sounds like airtight logic. Over and over the idea is stated and restated in various forms:

> *"Masturbation is sex with yourself."*
> *"Masturbation is just gratifying your own sexual needs."*
> *"Masturbation is indulging yourself."*

The list could go on. The basic core of these statements is that masturbation is wrong because it is self-centered and involves sexual pleasure.

"Quack!" It sounds like a duck. Why? Because we are told in Scripture that we are to deny ourselves and keep our fleshly desires in check. But tell me honestly: Is there any pleasure that *isn't* self-focused?

I do many things because they bring pleasure to me. I eat my favorite foods. I participate in a sport. I bring my wife flowers. I even serve the Lord because it brings me pleasure. It may be said that bringing flowers to my wife and serving the Lord brings pleasure to them also. This is true, but I do those things because they also bring me pleasure. My pleasure, among other things, becomes a motivator for my actions. Yet we often get the impression that anything involving personal pleasure, or motivated by personal pleasure, is sinful. First John 4:19 says that we love God and each other because God first loved us. By experiencing God's love, I love him in return. Personal, internal gratification becomes the prompt or motivator for loving God. Should John have been more careful not to reveal his selfish motives?

"I thought I needed to stop because God was punishing me by making my grandfather sick." —Mike, 23

We've already talked about the age-old battle the church has fought with Gnosticism, the philosophy that all matter is evil. Down through the centuries the church has also battled asceticism. This is the belief that all pleasure is evil and must be rejected. Asceticism reached great heights during monastic times, when monks would deny themselves everything from eating to speaking. (One poor fellow named Simeon Stylites sat on top of a stone pillar for thirty-six years, only requiring a few friends to bring him a little food and water each day. This was his way of avoiding sin, and he was fairly successful. But at what price?)

When these attempts failed, ascetics would often revert to self-mortification and inflict personal pain. Some people still hold to these views today, but most of us don't buy in. Yet when it comes to sexual issues, Satan keeps us in the bondage of asceticism.

I recently picked up a book by Dr. Erwin Lutzer, *Ten Lies About God and How You Might Already Be Deceived*. Lie number nine is that we think we must choose between God's pleasure and our pleasure.[3] We have the idea that we can't please ourselves because that wouldn't please God.

But it's not true. You see, because we are created in the image and like-ness of God, and because *he* receives pleasure, he created us to be pleasure-seeking beings. The idea that pleasure is always to be denied is a misinterpretation of God's Word and his desires for us. We can't rightly use the "pleasure myth" to call masturbation sin.

In fact, suppose we were to give thanks to God for every aspect of our physical bodies and their numerous processes? Have you ever tried that during your prayer time? I like what James B. Nelson, who writes on men's issues, has to say about this:

> *Insofar as our sexuality enters into our prayers at all, our first inclinations may be toward prayers of confession: for release from enslaving sexual desires; of guilt for wanting sex too much and making it the substitute for other things; for temptation or infidelity. The positive valuing of our bodies and our sexual experience may be more difficult, especially for men: thanksgiv-ing for the tastes, sounds, and smells that come through a sen-suous body; gratitude for grace known in orgasm. . . . Subjecting our genitals to oppression has made them subject to compulsions, and compulsions do not satisfy. . . . We do not need the crazy behavior of the slave let loose for the evening.*[4]

Okay, but . . . (and this is one of my occasional qualifying moments) can this get out of control?

Yes! While Dr. Lutzer never talks about masturbation, he does talk about seeking *lesser* pleasures. Lutzer says, "God who seeks pleasure created us so that we might do the same. Created in his image, we seek our own interests; we calculate what is best for us. God, however, is not led astray, and we are."[5] Often we settle for lesser pleasures than the highest pleasure of delighting in the Lord. God's Word says, "Delight yourself in the LORD and he will give you the desires of your heart" (Psalm 37:4).

As I type these words I'm sitting in the den in our basement. Upstairs my wife is playing a worship CD, and the song "Draw Me Close" fills the air. These words ring through the house:

> *You are my desire,*
> *no one else will do;*
> *'cause nothing else could take your place . . .*
> *You're all I want;*
> *You're all I've ever needed.*[6]

The highest pleasure is an intimate relationship with God. He is all we could ever want and he is all we need. When we delight in him, he instills in our heart the desires that it should have and then he fulfills those desires for our pleasure. Masturbation can be a sinful pleasure if it takes higher priority over the pleasure we find in God. Discerning the difference is the result of the Spirit's work in our lives.

THINK ABOUT IT!

1. In your own words, summarize the author's basic point about quacking ducks.

2. Which of the "Big Four M-Myths" has caused you the most trouble in the past? What new perspectives about them have you gained from reading this chapter?

3. Have you ever felt addicted to masturbation? What hope and/or encouragement have you found in this chapter's discussion of it?

4. What would you tell a close friend who says to you, "I guess all these troubles I'm having are payback from God"?

5. If you were to thank God for the pleasures in your life, what items would be on your top-five list? (Would you include sexual pleasure? Why or why not?)

CHAPTER FOUR

WHY IS MASTURBATION MOSTLY A "GUY THING"?

God is so cruel! He created men and women to reach their sexual peaks in their late adolescence—before they're married. What's up with that?

What was eighteenth-century philosopher Friedrich von Hardenberg talking about?

Most observers of the French Revolution, especially the clever and noble ones, have explained it as a life-threatening and contagious illness. They have remained standing with the symptoms and have interpreted these in manifold and contrary ways. Some have regarded it as a merely local ill. The most ingenious opponents have pressed for castration. They well noticed that this alleged illness is nothing other than the crisis of . . . beginning puberty.[1]

Ah, puberty! Remember it?

You may not have caused a national revolution or changed the course of world events when you started growing hair under your arms. Nevertheless, for you—as it is for every human being—puberty was a *really big deal!*

Obviously, our excitable German thinker went a bit far with his claim about puberty's cosmic effects. But you have to admit that it was (or is) a time in your life when everything seemed to go completely haywire. And why not? Puberty unleashes some major physiological changes.

THE ANATOMICAL REVOLUTION BEGINS

At no time in human development is physical growth so pronounced and dramatic. It all starts when your body turns on a flood of hormones called *gonadotropins*. Simply put, gonadotropins are sex hormones. The body produces many different kinds, but the primary ones are testosterone, estrogen, and progesterone. The male body produces mostly testosterone, while the female body produces mostly estrogen and progesterone. Somewhere between the ages of seven to twelve a child's body will start to release gonadotropins into the bloodstream. (Don't get hung up on the timing, though. Puberty kicks in at different times for different people. As *The Complete Book of Guys* writer, Dave Barry, said: "I reached puberty at age thirty. At age twelve I looked like a fetus." Now you don't feel so bad, right?)

Anyway . . . this hormone release gets triggered by the activity of the pituitary gland and the hypothalamus, both located at the base of the brain. This is a good time to make one thing clear: Our primary sex organ is the brain. The brain controls sexual impulses, sexual thoughts, sexual drives, and sexual function. This is critical to remember when we start to discuss things like lust. Brain function, under God's timing, turns on a slow stream of these hormones.

The first effect they have on a person's body is to generate bone growth. Gonadotropins activate the bone-growth center, and the child starts to experience growth spurts. His hands and feet become bigger first because smaller bones are primarily and more easily affected by these gonadotropins. As these hormones do their job, the child starts to grow in stature. Sex hormones in prepubescence (and through the duration of adolescence) will be responsible for physiological growth as well as sexological development.

Eventually the preteen begins to grow taller, and just when starting to "grow out of his or her clothes," the person begins to develop sexually. How ironic! God certainly has a sense of humor. God sort of opens the hormone faucet a little more, as the hypothalamus begins to produce a gonadotropin-releasing hormone that activates the development of the ovaries and the testicles. When this happens, the testicles in the male start the production of more testosterone as well as sperm and semen. The ovaries in the female start to produce estrogen and progesterone, which will be responsible to mature at least one ovum every month out of the hundreds that her body has carried since birth. Estrogen and progesterone will also control and regulate the girl's menstrual cycle.

AND THE TENSION BUILDS

At this point you're probably wondering, *Is this going somewhere, Steve?* Yes—stick with me here. You see, those hormones, which are doing their job to make a kid physiologically mature and sexually developed, are the same hormones that regulate sex drive and desires. They are the hormones that give us our sexual appetite. They're the hormones that make us . . . well, "horny"—there's really no other word for it.

My point is that adolescents (ages eleven to twenty-three) depend on these sex hormones for physical growth *as well as sexual development.* Apart from the physical growth and development created by these sex hormones, they have the same effect on the mind and body of an adolescent as they do on an adult. Think about it: These hormones turn those adolescent bodies on, sexually. Adolescents experience all the sexual desires, drives, tensions, and needs (maybe even more intensely) that an adult does.

When a guy's body starts to manufacture testosterone, his sex drive increases dramatically. (Testosterone is the hormone responsible for sexual drives in both the male and female, but it's the primary gonadotropin produced in a guy's body.) When this happens, he experiences frequent and often uncontrolled erections. His body begins to produce sperm and semen in great amounts. A cycle begins to develop here. As his body releases testosterone to produce sperm and semen, it will also induce a strong sexual appetite. Basically, his body begins to urge him to do something about the sperm and semen that his body stores.

Now, if you're this guy, you have one of four options to eliminate this seminal buildup:

1. *You just let it go away on its own.* Yes, it will dissipate within your body, all by itself. The sperm can die off and disintegrate, or dissolve. It will be reabsorbed into your system. This process takes a long time because the sperm cells can have a long lifespan. This option usually isn't very effective in adolescents and young men because their bodies can produce sperm faster than the sperm die off.

2. *You decide to tie the knot.* Another way a young man can eliminate semen buildup is through sexual intercourse. Of course, for committed Christian guys, this means getting married and settling down. This isn't usually filling the minds of early adolescents, but it soon becomes a part of their thinking in middle and later adolescence. We know and teach the biblical and moral standards regarding premarital sexual intercourse. Therefore, many young men choose not to be sexually active because of their values and

convictions. Thus, elimination of the buildup of sperm and semen through intercourse ceases to be an option until marriage.

3. *You sleep — and hope.* The third way a guy's body can find relief from the physical sexual tension is through a *nocturnal emission,* or what is commonly called a "wet dream." This can be anything from a slow emission that occurs while a guy is asleep to a vivid, erotic sexual fantasy played out in his dream until orgasm. When a guy experiences a slow emission, he may not wake up but will just find himself and his bed wet in the morning. When a guy experiences a mature wet dream, the orgasm and ejaculation often awaken him.

Many people who hold an anti-masturbation stance believe that this is the God-given way of release and therefore masturbation should be avoided. The problem with this view is that only a small population of men experience frequent nocturnal emissions. Some men experience them regularly, but this is rare. Some men experience them occasionally, meaning only a few times in the course of a year. Others can count the number of times over several decades, while some have never experienced a wet dream at all.

"I have more guilt over sexual dreams than over masturbation because I can control my thoughts when I masturbate, but I can't when I'm having a dream. When I see the girl who was in my dream, it makes me feel really awkward and ashamed." — **Brian, 22**

While a nocturnal emission is a normal thing, it isn't a frequent, common experience among men. I've talked with guys who were told, "If you stop masturbating, then God will allow you to have wet dreams." Some of those guys say this happens, but not with regularity.

I have a few students who call it "the gift." That way, they can talk in code: "Hey, I got a gift last night, did you?"

Others struggle all the more because they don't experience this thing that they were told God would provide for them. They wait for "the gift," but they never get it. I have even talked to some guys who masturbate and experience wet dreams too! The truth is, there's no standardization to the wet-dream experience. Just because a guy doesn't masturbate doesn't insure that he will have wet dreams.

There is a lot of confusion around the issue of nocturnal emissions. Most anti-masturbation theorists seem to be all in favor of wet dreams. Their reasoning is that a wet dream can't be controlled, so God must be allowing it (or at least he'll be more tolerant of it). They write off the full erotic dream experience as *not* being sexual fantasy or lust. The trouble with this is that both forms of arousal stem from the same place—the mind. They accomplish the same result—self-pleasurable orgasmic sexual relief. The only difference is that in one state the person is consciously controlling it while in the other he is not. (We'll talk more about this when we deal with sexual thinking and sexual lust in chapter 6.)

Let's recap. Physically, a guy's body can eliminate sperm and semen through natural dissipation, which doesn't happen fast enough in many adolescents; through sexual intercourse, which has clearly defined biblical and moral boundaries; or through wet dreams, which aren't as common as we're led to believe.

Then there's the fourth way.

4. *You take matters into your own hands.* This is the fourth option for release: You masturbate. Now, all of the discussion so far in this chapter has been building up to one main question. I wanted to

raise it at the very beginning, but I needed to lay a physiological foundation first. Here's the question that a lot of guys wonder about: Why do men masturbate more than women? That is, exactly *why* is this so much of a "guy thing"?

Remember those gonadotropins? Well, the release of these totally annoying hormones into your system, which creates your raging urge for sex, may be God's way of letting a guy's body notify him that *something must be done.*

This may be one reason why masturbation is more common to men than to women. It fulfills a physiological need in men that women don't have. It may also be a reason why masturbation is more "instinctual" for men: It becomes the release from seminal buildup.[2]

With the physiological information you now have, you're fairly clued-in to some answers. But the question isn't just an intellectual curiosity. No, that's why the second half of this chapter is important. You see, the question is also, in a sense, a "complaint." Maybe that's too strong a word for it, but in the minds of most of us men, there might linger a little bit of resentment about why we guys have to struggle so much with masturbation.

THE LIST OF GRIEVANCES

In fact, I can think of at least five related types of grievances that guys have voiced to me over the years, either in personal counseling or just in friendly talks. Maybe you'll find one or two of your own here. If so, I hope my responses help—or maybe they'll help you help a friend down the road.

"Why do girls get all the breaks?"

Isn't it terribly unfair that men get strapped with this constant physiological urge, while females, in general, have less of a purely physical drive for release? It's the pits!

There are all kinds of competing statistics about what percentage of guys masturbate and what percentage of girls masturbate. Regardless of the exact stats, one thing is clear: An overwhelming majority of men do it, whereas slightly less than half of the female population does it. This would lead us to believe that masturbation is a guy thing. The truth is that it's not *solely* a guy thing, but more physiological factors play into making it a predominantly male activity. To fully understand this, we need to jump back into some basic physiological facts — and also point out that women have their own sexuality challenges too.

For example, you might know that many women have difficulty with their menstrual cycles. They can often experience cramping during the premenstrual and ovulatory stage of their cycles, right before they actually start their menstrual flow. But did you know that masturbation can help relieve these cramps? Once again, the body creates a natural pain and stress reliever in the adrenalines released during orgasm. Some women are encouraged by their doctors to masturbate as a form of relief.

Women who experience pain during intercourse (called dyspareunia) are often encouraged to masturbate as well. This accomplishes two things. First, it makes her more aware of her body. She is able to discover how her body functions and responds to touch and stimulation. Second, it makes her more relaxed. The pain often results from a tightening or spasm of the muscles surrounding the vagina. Masturbation helps a woman train her body to relax.

So there are legitimate, natural physiological factors that play into making an informed decision about masturbation. But to say that "because something is natural then it is acceptable"? That's a big leap; sin is natural too.

On the other hand, to dismiss masturbation as being a totally abnormal phenomenon is not accurate. Masturbation can be a good thing because of the physiological effects that accompany it. Masturbation, like any another physiological function, can't be separated from other issues. Eating is a physiological function. In and of itself we would say that it is necessary for good health. But we realize that is simplistic. We can overeat, eat the wrong things, or eat to addiction. So we formulate values and convictions about eating. For example, we can feast in order to celebrate, and we find that occasionally acceptable. Or we can sometimes fast, in the light of the rest of the world's hunger. In other words, a simple physiological act can take on greater meaning in the light of our moral point of view. The same is true of masturbation.

"What about those 'man-cramps'?" Or, to put it another way: "Is 'blue-ball' real?"
Yes. If a young guy doesn't have frequent wet dreams and isn't having intercourse or masturbating regularly, he may experience some physical discomfort. This actual disorder is commonly called blue-ball. Doctors don't have a technical term for this phenomenon because they can't specifically pinpoint its causes—nor agree on exactly what it is. It seems to be an umbrella term that encompasses minor groin and testicular pain. Many guys talk about having this pain after they've had a date or been in a romantic encounter. Maybe it happens because those sexually charged experiences make his body ready for sex. But then . . . no sex!

Some men report experiencing the same groin pain when they haven't had a wet dream or experienced an ejaculation for a long time. Most physicians think that it occurs when sexual arousal is prolonged without release.

When a male is aroused, his penis engorges with blood. The process will subside if arousal is minimized. But if he maintains that erection for a long period of time, he will experience discomfort. Many guys find relief from it when they masturbate. One reason for this may be due to the simple process of orgasm. When orgasm occurs, the body's drive and hormonal surge subsides.

Men may also experience a disorder known as *prostatitis*. The prostate gland, which produces ejaculatory fluids, becomes inflamed. Prostatitis has many different stages, which can range from swelling to infection. Regardless of the type of prostatitis, as a part of the treatment plan many urologists believe that frequent ejaculation (sometimes two to three times weekly) helps to eliminate the problem and quicken recovery.[3]

Many of these physicians also believe that regular ejaculation will serve as a preventive measure against the onset of prostatitis. While no medical professional or text is quick to say conclusively that fluids build up in the prostate, they give the impression that it's possible. With that in mind, it could be that the need for elimination of these seminal fluids becomes a God-instilled response. This may be another physiological reason why masturbation is more of a guy thing than a girl thing. (In addition, it may also point to some health benefits of masturbation for unmarried men who don't compromise their moral stance with sexual promiscuity.)

"Why is God so cruel to us guys?"

Guys might ask this question when they think about the irony of the Sexual Peak. One high school student said to me, "God is so cruel! He created men and women to reach their sexual peaks in their late adolescence—before they're married. What's up with *that?*" Almost weekly this guy would have this discussion with me. The problem was that he misinterpreted what "sexual peaking" actually means.

When a late adolescent (ages eighteen to twenty-three) nears the end of his or her sexological and physical development, the gonadotropins used to generate this growth will no longer be needed for that part of development. Those hormones will take up their roles in the ongoing sexual health and response of that individual's body. This means those hormones will be responsible for sperm and semen production, ovulation and menstruation, and sexual urges and drives. But they won't be needed for bone and muscle growth and development.

As a way of shutting down the process, God opens the floodgates on these hormones. He overloads the system so that it creates a kind of circuit-breaker effect that shuts down the bone growth centers. So, at this sexual-peak point, an individual may frequently be more easily and intensely aroused.

Many late adolescent guys have wept over the fact that they've prayed and prayed for God to help them control their sexual thoughts. They begin to doubt that God is keeping his promise to answer prayer! Why isn't God cooling down their ferocious sex drives? They question their walk with God because they are so easily and often aroused. They become completely discouraged because they masturbate more frequently to avoid physical pain or the embarrassment of spontaneously ejaculating in their pants when their girlfriends kiss them or affectionately touch them. (By the way, many men have had an experience like that.) That poor guy begins to believe he's a sexual pervert, so he runs to God again and asks God to take it all away.

God isn't going to take it away. He has wired our bodies most wonderfully. He's keeping us healthy by allowing this hormonal surge. If it
didn't happen, we'd never stop growing. God isn't turning a deaf ear to
those prayers; he is indeed answering them. And some think that controlled masturbation is God's answer to getting through this tough
time.

"Why does the first time have to be such a shock?"

It's difficult to resist saying that, for many guys, "first ejaculation and
masturbation go hand in hand." (I know that's a lame pun, but it's true.)
Many men experienced their first ejaculation during a mild masturbation experience like washing themselves or fondling themselves. For
many guys this is a surprising, and even traumatic, event.

**"The first time I did it I came out of my bedroom and sat on
the couch in a daze. My eyes must have been glassy because
my dad asked me if I was on drugs."** —Justin, 21

As kids we hear about where babies come from. We learn the
basics about conception and contraception. We often aren't told the
mechanics of sex, and we suffer big informational gaps, especially
when it starts to affect us personally. For example, prepubescent and
junior-high girls are often forewarned and prepared about having their
first period. This wasn't always the case. Menstruation was once
viewed as a shamefully private thing, just like masturbation. At one
time girls were simply informed that they'd have "a monthly visitor,"
and nothing more was said. When a girl had her period, she was
caught off guard, and the process was quite traumatic. Mothers were
often embarrassed to talk to their daughters until it was too late.
Thankfully, women today have overcome the shame, and today girls
know about their periods prior to having them. They are coached

through the process by their mothers, sisters, or other nurturing women. Menstruation is no longer a surprise, and the shame of something so natural fades away.

What about a guy? At some point he's going to experience his first ejaculation. This may occur during a wet dream, but it is most likely going to occur during some form of genital contact due to the hormonal surge. We tell prepubescent and junior-high guys that they may experience this thing called a wet dream. We don't describe what it is, but it doesn't matter because they ejaculate prior to having one. These boys think that a wet dream is the way they will experience this thing called ejaculation (by the way, we rarely tell them how that works either). They find themselves in a shower or some other setting where they are masturbating. The end result is that they ejaculate.

Then what do they do? I've had many guys tell me they had no idea what had just happened. I can relate. You've just had this outrageous feeling accompanied by a discharge that you've never seen before. You know it's not blood, because it's white, but you're pretty sure you broke something because you just experienced this uncontrolled spurting. But it doesn't hurt, either.

"My parents bought me a book about the birds and bees, so the first time I experienced an ejaculation I kind of knew what was going on. But I wasn't sure." —Paul, 19

So how do you find out about this? All your life you've been receiving messages about "not touching yourself." You might think, "God's punishing me," but you can't find out about it either. How are you going to talk about this? You can't come out and say what you were doing. So you wait. The next day you're okay; you didn't die.

Then you remember the feeling of orgasm. The process repeats itself, and you piece together the physiological facts of your experience, maybe from locker-room conversations. You come to the conclusion that what you experienced was an ejaculation.

Go figure . . . you've become a man!

"Why am I sexually sabotaged — at the worst times?"

Masturbation does have a relation to stress. One college-age guy named Roger told me:

> *Steve, I'm convinced that masturbation is sabotaging my life. I try all week to go without doing it. I work hard to keep my mind off sex by getting real involved in other stuff — I've got sports, classes, homework, a job, and I work with the junior-high youth group.*
>
> *But at the end of the week, when I'm alone and don't have all those distractions . . . well, I just give in. This whole struggle is like a battle I'm fighting; it just drains me of energy. It's like I'm set up for failure. And maybe God is taking away my vitality as a consequence.*

Roger's focus on "staying away from himself" all week was consuming him. The stress related to keeping control left him with little resistance. He also added a sense of self-defeat on top of the physiological effect — and that emotionally and spiritually immobilized him as well.

But here's another way to look at it: What this young guy had discovered was *the relaxing, stress-relieving effect of orgasm.* Many men and women have said that masturbation helps them sleep better or brings physical relief from stress. That is true; it can and does. The body produces endorphins that act as calming agents. During orgasm a person experiences an endorphin rush. This relieves physical stress.

Some of you may be thinking . . .

But doesn't God relieve stress?
Shouldn't we be in prayer about the stressors of life?
Isn't dependence on masturbation for stress relief the beginning
of an addiction?

The answer could be yes to all of those questions—but it is not universally yes. God is no less involved if the person who is looking to him for stress relief finds it in what God has already provided through the outlet of orgasm. Many who experience this outlet through masturbation as a stress reliever say it is little different, and no more addicting, than the routine of a good run or workout. The effects are the same. But if there is to be standardization, it must be applied consistently across the board.

"Sometimes I feel like I'm going to explode; I try not to think about sexual things, and I avoid any sexual stuff. But my hormones get out of control. When I do the big M, all that goes away fast." —Ben, 17

One thing is certain: We all experience deep desire and a lifelong search for nurture. One Christian writer even said, "Spirituality is what we do with our desire."[4] Our question has been: Does masturbation have its legitimate place in this very human situation?

We've looked at some of the physiological data that may point us toward an answer. Now it's time to look more deeply into the Bible, the focus of our next chapter.

THINK ABOUT IT!

1. What new information did you learn in this chapter about the physiology of sex?

2. Why would the author say: "Our primary sex organ is the brain"? Do you agree?

3. Which of the five "complaint" subheadings hits closest to home for you? Why?

4. What other complaint would you add to this chapter, based on your own experience?

5. What are your thoughts about God's role in your sexual development and functioning? Has he ever seemed unfair to you? Or particularly gracious? (If you're studying this book in a group, talk about it!)

CHAPTER FIVE

DOES THE BIBLE TALK ABOUT, YOU KNOW . . . "IT"?

I've always been taught that the Old Testament specifically forbids masturbation. But I know Christ came to fulfill the Law, and the church is under grace anyway.

A friend jokingly commented that she always wanted to write a book titled *Everything the Bible Says About Masturbation.* It would consist entirely of blank pages.

But it would be an accurate book. The Bible just doesn't address masturbation. It specifically deals with many other sexual themes, such as adultery, fornication, incest, rape, homosexuality, and even zoophilia (sex with animals). It outlines specific rites and rituals for Israel concerning childbirth, menstruation, and nocturnal emissions. It gives detailed guidelines about marriage and celibacy—and enthusiastically celebrates the joy of sex.

But masturbation? Not a word.

The Bible's silence here is significant. Some have said it means that masturbation is morally acceptable. Others assume it indicates immoral behavior. But, of course, neither side can use the direct words of Scripture to make its point.

However, certain Christians through the ages have tried to show that masturbation is wrong by taking Scripture out of context. These people have believed that the Bible either speaks *directly* or *indirectly* to the issue. Many have gone so far as to manipulate Scripture to produce "proof texts."

In this chapter, we'll look at some of the often-used biblical texts to see how this has been done. I hope you'll have your Bible open as we go, and that you'll prayerfully seek God's guidance for your own life. We'll begin our Scripture study with a guy who was banking on getting away with some serious deception.

POOR ONAN: BIG PENALTY FOR EARLY WITHDRAWAL! (SEE GENESIS 38:6-10)

The first attempts to prove that masturbation is immoral drew upon a story in the Old Testament, in Genesis 38. The passage says that a man named Onan "spilled his semen on the ground" (verse 9), and thus was judged severely with "death by God."

Men like Tissot, Graham, and Kellogg—along with their contemporary medical and religious leaders—interpreted Onan's actions as masturbatory. For them, here was the definitive proof text that God was so anti-masturbation that he punished it by wiping the guy out. This supported their beliefs that masturbation was at the root of all diseases, because death was inevitable if you masturbated.

"I think the Bible somewhere says that masturbation is a sin. Doesn't one of the prophets talk about it?"   —Ben, 17

For hundreds of years, this text stood as the Bible's supposed condemnation of "self-abuse." People believed the passage spoke so clearly against the sin of masturbation that they began to call masturbation by what they made to be the biblical term *onanism*, after Onan's sin. Many today still believe this text stands as proof of an abominable sin to the Lord. Let's look a little closer, though, at what the Bible actually says (and *doesn't* say). The story reads:

> *Judah got a wife for Er, his firstborn, and her name was Tamar. But Er, Judah's firstborn, was wicked in the LORD's sight; so the LORD put him to death. Then Judah said to Onan, "Lie with your brother's wife and fulfill your duty to her as a brother-in-law to produce offspring for your brother." But Onan knew that the offspring would not be his; so whenever he lay with his brother's wife, he spilled his semen on the ground to keep from producing offspring for his brother. What he did was wicked in the LORD's sight; so he put him to death also. (Genesis 38:6-10)*

Now let's unpack the story. Onan was the younger brother of Er. Er had married a woman named Tamar. Er was also the firstborn of his father, Judah, putting him in the position of being the family patriarch. This meant that he would be responsible for the financial, relational, and spiritual well-being of the family, because in those days the patriarch was the family leader, priest, ruler, CEO, and king (so to speak).

One of Er's responsibilities was to have a son to succeed him as patriarch and keep Judah's lineage pure and unbroken. Before Er could complete this task, he died, leaving his wife, Tamar, barren. Here's where Onan enters the story. You see, there was a rule that if the patriarchal successor died without leaving a male heir, the younger brother of the successor should have sex with his sister-in-law for the purpose of providing a male offspring who would carry on the dead brother's name and lineage. If the dead brother happened to be the next patriarch, then the son, by the living brother, would become the family patriarch. This rule would become known as the "Levirate law" (see Deuteronomy 25:5-10).[1]

Now here's where it gets complicated—as if it isn't already! The brother, Onan in this case, was to have sexual relations only to impregnate his sister-in-law, Tamar. The male child that he produced would then become patriarch, keeping his older brother's—in this case Er and his father, Judah's—lineage intact. That meant that all authority, wealth, and rule went to this child.

So what? Well, the catch was that the younger brother (Onan) was also responsible to support that child in every way—having all the responsibility but no privileges of patriarchy. All of the family inheritance and rule would go to the child he sired. Onan would be making a huge sacrifice in this way, thus redeeming his brother's lineage and patriarchal succession. The younger brother in this type of situation would be called *goel* in Hebrew, or "kinsman redeemer." As kinsman redeemer he would ultimately reflect a picture of Christ. Israel would be reminded from the example of the *goel* that Messiah would come to redeem his "kin," his people. Onan knew this and he knew that the child "would not be his" (verse 9).

Here's where the plot thickens. According to the customs of that day, if Onan couldn't provide a male offspring, then the line of patriarchy would shift directly to him as the next-born male son of the patriarch (Judah).

So Onan decided to deceive.

He wanted everyone to think that he was doing his duty as the *goel*, but he didn't want to impregnate Tamar. Onan saw his opportunity to seize the patriarchy. He faked orgasm (yes, men can fake it too) and withdrew before orgasm occurred, thus spilling his seed on the ground. This sexual act is known as *coitus interruptus*. My point: If there is a sexual sin to be judged here, it would be coitus interruptus, not masturbation.

But God didn't judge Onan for any sexual sin. He judged Onan for his trickery and unfaithfulness. Onan's deceit lead Tamar and everyone else to believe that he had done the job. It was perceived that poor Tamar couldn't get pregnant and that Onan so wonderfully and graciously sacrificed his shot at the patriarchy. There would be no other recourse but to give the birthright and patriarchal lineage to Onan.

Tamar didn't believe she was barren, however. So she disguised herself as a prostitute and had sex with her father-in-law, Judah. (Prostitutes were veiled, so she was able to conceal her identity during the act of intercourse.) Judah was the only other option for her to preserve a direct and pure lineage. She became pregnant and had a male child. According to the law, she risked losing her life for her infidelity but God honored her for her sacrificial act.

There was a lot at stake here because the line of Judah was the line that God chose to bring Messiah into the world. It was the pure line that Jesus would be born into, and Tamar is one of three women mentioned in that lineage (see Matthew 1:3). Each woman mentioned put herself at great risk to preserve the line and was thus honored by God.

But God took Onan's life for his despicable act of deception and greed. Onan was messing with God's eternally designed plan, violating the lineage of the Royal line. King David would come from the line of Judah, and so would Messiah. How this becomes a proof text against masturbation is hard to understand, given the context. In addition, consider all the sexually questionable things occurring in this story but never addressed by the anti-onanism crusaders. They singled out an incidental phrase and built an entire moral theory around it. This is a clear example of misusing Scripture. The story of Onan is not about masturbation.

THE OLD TESTAMENT LAW: LET'S KEEP IT CLEAN, GUYS (SEE LEVITICUS 15:16-18)

A college student once confided: "I've always been taught that the Old Testament Law specifically forbids masturbation. But I know Christ came to fulfill the Law, and the church is under grace anyway. So it really doesn't matter if the Old Testament forbids masturbation."

I had a few problems with his comment. I reminded him that just because Christ fulfilled the Law, doesn't mean the Law doesn't serve as a moral guide for us. It also doesn't mean that we can do as we please. If that were the case, then murder, adultery, theft—all forbidden by the Law—would be acceptable. God's law is still intact. What Christ fulfilled and delivered us from was the *penalty* of the Law; therefore, we are under grace.

After we cleared this up, I was still curious to know where he thought the Law "specifically forbids masturbation." He took me to a text often used to support that view:

> *"'If a man has a seminal emission, he shall bathe all his body in water and be unclean until evening. As for any garment or any leather on which there is seminal emission, it shall be washed with water and be unclean until evening. If a man lies with a woman so that there is a seminal emission, they shall both bathe in water and be unclean until evening.'"* (Leviticus 15:16-18, NASB)

This passage does talk about seminal discharge—which would include masturbation—but is not *restricted* to masturbation. Before we can understand what's being said in these verses, we must look at the passages preceding it. Moses wrote rules that governed normal and abnormal conditions. The *abnormal* conditions involved sexual disease that brought on seminal discharge. Such diseases would have included venereal diseases. The discharge from these diseases made the person unclean, thus requiring ceremonial cleansing, offerings of atonement, and an eventual appointment with the priest to prove one's cure. This was the procedure for virtually any other disease. After Jesus healed the man with leprosy (see Luke 5:12-14), he commanded the man to follow the instructions given in the Law.

The *normal* discharge didn't involve an offering for sin. However, normal seminal discharge was also considered unclean because the natural procreative fluids reminded people that sin was transferred from generation to generation through birth. The act of being made clean would stress that they needed God to deliver them from a sinful nature.

The law doesn't distinguish how the seminal discharge occurs. This cleansing ritual would have taken place after intercourse, after a wet dream, or even after masturbation. To imply that this passage means masturbation is sinful is a misinterpretation. This same ritual is required of women after menstruation (see Leviticus 15:19-24). We don't read that a woman having her period is in sin, do we?

This text supposedly supported the idea that masturbation was a cause of disease, as well. Those good old doctors of yesteryear focused particularly on spermatorrhea, an excessive or uncontrolled discharge of semen. This text seemed to harmonize with their medical ignorance. Yet it no more implies that masturbation is sinful than it does that orgasm is sinful.

SOLO SEX: NATURALLY, *UNNATURAL?* (SEE ROMANS 1)

When I was working as a counselor, I met with one high school guy, Tim, who seemed depressed. I wanted to check for symptoms, so I began asking a series of questions. Often, when a depression is severe, a person will lose appetite. And loss of appetite doesn't only involve food but also sex drive.

As I probed, I asked him about masturbation. If masturbation (or any sexual activity, for that matter) was a common practice, and there was a significant decrease in its frequency, then this would also indicate a loss of appetite. He responded, "I never, *ever* do that, because it's not natural!"

"What do you mean, Tim?"

"Well, I've always been told that it's kind of weird for anybody to *like* touching themselves. I mean, if a guy likes *that* so much, maybe he's gay—or maybe he's gonna *become* gay. So I just don't do it."

"But what about all the sexual tension that builds up?"

"Ah, I guess you need to get somebody of the opposite sex to do it for you. At least that's, like, *normal.*"

Tim's views aren't all that uncommon. Many people believe masturbation isn't natural, though they rarely define what "natural" means. Most of the time the implication is that masturbation doesn't fulfill God's design for marriage. The verse often used to support this view is Romans 1:27, where sinful men and women exchanged what was natural for that which was unnatural. As a result, God gave them over to the depravity of their hearts and minds.

"I always believed that whenever the Bible talked about sinful desires it meant sexual desires. I couldn't think of any sexual desire that wasn't sinful." —Brian, 22

Again, delve into the context. Recall that Paul was writing to the Romans, who were wrestling with how salvation works in the light of their sinful desires. Paul started by unfolding the story of sin at the beginning. He argued that we were *naturally* created without sin and in fellowship with God. But sin entered the picture, and human beings chose to ignore God and rebel against him. God continues to reveal himself to all people, even through nature (see verse 20). They therefore have no excuse for rejecting him outright.

Mankind chooses to reject him, though, and as a result God gives them over to their impure, lustful hearts (see verse 24), degrading passions (see verse 26), and a depraved mind (see verse 28). That which was natural becomes the unnatural. Paul continued to illustrate this by talking about the sin of homosexuality.

Some use the "argument of design" to say that masturbation is unnatural. They say sex was designed for two, a man and a woman. This view doesn't necessarily use the Romans 1 passage as a proof text, but it becomes the springboard to support the argument. Someone who holds to this view would say that the illustrations, principles, and moral values pertaining to sexuality in the Bible have a specific relational and procreative design. Therefore, masturbation doesn't fit the original design.

Those who hold this view would say that "self-sex" or "solo sex" isn't mentioned in Scripture and runs counter to the way God designed sex. (By the way, the idea of solo sex was popularized by comedian Woody Allen, who said, "Hey, don't knock masturbation; it's sex with someone I love.") This view assumes that masturbation is, in fact, sex with oneself. Others would say that is ridiculous, agreeing that sex is designed to be between two people. These people would argue that while masturbation is a part of sexuality, it is no more a relational sex act than menstruation. They would agree that sex is designed to be a relational act between two people. And they would continue to say that drawing conclusions that masturbation is a relational sex act is where the argument of design breaks down and false assumptions arise. Nobody can have sex with himself or herself. These people would argue, then, that masturbation is a natural function designed for many purposes, such as helping an individual understand his or her body's natural abilities or helping one overcome sexual temptation.

The argument from design advances further when proponents point out that masturbation has no procreative value. This carries a lot of old baggage—the assumption that anything sexual must have procreative value and must be void of pleasure. But God's design for sex obviously does involve pleasure as well as procreation. If this were not true, then those who hold to a procreative design argument would have to apply the same argument to other sexual issues, such as oral sex and even contraception. The books of Proverbs and Song of Solomon make it clear that sexual pleasure is a part of God's design for sex.

For all practical purposes one could argue that masturbation is more natural than unnatural. Many studies conclude that masturbation is instinctual. Children discover that touching themselves brings pleasure while it also helps them acquire knowledge about the wonderful design of their bodies. Some studies show that masturbation may even occur while the child is in the womb. Instinct implies some form of naturalness.

There are studies showing that masturbation helps women who experience anorgasmia (the inability to achieve orgasm) and dyspareunia (pain during intercourse). Masturbation also helps a man experiencing premature ejaculation to overcome that problem. This "natural remedy" may be preferable to other medical options.

But suppose we were to concede, just for the sake of argument, that masturbation is unnatural. Why should we then assume that because something runs counter to design it automatically makes that thing evil? Think of all the things that are "unnatural" and are also very good, such as intravenous feeding, blood transfusions, or artificial respirators. Driving a car is not a natural means of transportation, and flying defies everything that is natural; however, we don't see these things as evil merely because they run counter to the design of gravity. Scripture is silent on all of these issues too.

We also see many things in Scripture that are "unnatural," yet we don't label those as evil. For example, there's nothing natural about miracles or a virgin birth! Healing on the Sabbath ran counter to design, as did eating meat sacrificed to idols. So if you argue that something is wrong because it runs counter to design, then you would have to apply that view consistently to everything. And that's tough to do.

BETTER TO MARRY THAN MASTURBATE?
(SEE 1 CORINTHIANS 7:9)

I once heard a pastor speaking on sexuality, and his message was excellent. He seemed to be handling Scripture accurately. But as an aside, he briefly commented on masturbation. His entire proof that God despised masturbation flowed from the premise that God commands marriage as the "relief from sexual burning." He went on to say: "The Bible tells us that it's better to *marry* than to burn; it does not say that it's better to *masturbate* than to burn." He was referring to these verses:

> *To the unmarried and the widows I say: It is good for them to*
> *stay unmarried, as I am. But if they cannot control themselves,*

they should marry, for it is better to marry than to burn with
passion. (1 Corinthians 7:8-9)

To single out one verse to support a position, without looking at it in the context of the entire passage, skews the meaning. In this passage Paul answered some questions regarding marriage, sexual contact, and celibacy for the Corinthian believers. We don't know exactly what those questions were; we just know that Paul started by saying, "Now for the matters you wrote about" (verse 1).

Obviously, they had some questions about their natural passions as well as how the whole sex, marriage, and celibacy thing works in the light of pleasing and serving God. Paul would build a case later in the chapter that unmarried folks can be more focused on serving God because their priorities aren't divided. Married people who serve the Lord must also serve their spouses. Paul was clear throughout his teaching that he thought celibacy is less complicating and the better option. He even said to the unmarried and widows that "it is good for them to stay unmarried, as I am" (verse 8).

Most Bible scholars believe Paul was single. His preference in this passage is that singles remain unmarried. On the other hand, Paul also realized that celibacy is a gift from God and that not everyone possesses that gift (see verse 7). Paul made it clear that if a person has strong sexual urges he is free to get married and not fight those urges. And how do you know whether you have the gift of celibacy? It's simple; if you're constantly burning with passion then you don't have the gift!

Some scholars note that the phrase "cannot control themselves," found in verse 9, is not in the Bible's original Greek text. These scholars believe Paul was referring back to verse 1 of this passage, indicating that those who have no self-control—*and* are already engaged in sexual contact (some translations say "touching" a woman)—should marry. The more accurate translation is "if they are not living" morally pure they should marry rather than fight their burning passion.[2]

This passage focuses on the married state versus the unmarried state. Paul was giving guidelines to help the Corinthian believers make that decision. *Never did he mention masturbation.* Yet this would have been a good place for Paul to address masturbation if it were universally regarded as sin. He didn't, even though he specifically addressed various sexual sins throughout all of his epistles. Clearly, the text speaks neither for nor against masturbation.

LUST: ALWAYS TIED TO THE "BIG M"?
(SEE MATTHEW 5:27-28)

Those who use this passage remark that masturbation involves lusting. And while masturbation is never specifically mentioned as sin in the Bible, lust is. This passage then becomes clear proof that masturbation, with its inseparable partner, lust, is condemned by Jesus. The passage reads:

> *You have heard that it was said, "YOU SHALL NOT COMMIT*
> *ADULTERY"; but I say to you that everyone who looks at a*
> *woman with lust for her has already committed adultery with*
> *her in his heart. (Matthew 5:27-28, NASB)*

Those who use this passage as an anti-masturbatory text often deduce that masturbation involves working out strong sexual urges, desires, thoughts, and agendas that culminate in orgasm. They make the assumption that these urges, desires, thoughts, and agendas are what Jesus means by "lust." That is, masturbation can't occur apart from lust and it is therefore wrong. (Before we get too involved in looking at the interpretation of this text, it's important to say that masturbation may very well be connected directly to the sin of lust . . . for *some* people. It is not universal.)

We must treat this passage with great integrity. Jesus was making a specific point to a specific group of people. He was speaking to Jews who believed they were acceptable to God because of their birth status as Hebrews and because they (supposedly) had not broken the Law. Jesus used the phrase "You have heard it said . . . but I say to you" a number of times in this sermon. By doing that he's claiming deity and the absolute authority to reinterpret the Law. He stressed that the *intent of the heart* is as sinful as the act itself. A person may not have committed an act of adultery, but if he has entertained lustful thoughts, he's as guilty as if he committed the physical act.

"I assumed it was wrong because growing up in a Christian home you get the impression that all sexual things are wrong and that the Bible just talks about sex as a bad thing."
—Paul, 19

If the passage stopped at this point, then it could support the view that masturbation is wrong. One would be hard-pressed to argue that masturbation can happen without sexual thinking, although some have tried to assert that it can. With this incomplete context of the passage we would have to agree that lusting about sex, accompanied by masturbation, is wrong.

But there is much more to consider.

We need to understand the intent of Jesus' words. Was he talking about sexual thinking when he used the word *lust?* Did he mean that strong sexual drive and "dwelling" on those thoughts was equal to the act? Just what does it mean?

I once heard a youth pastor say that lust was "a strong desire to acquire something that isn't yours." But that's how I got my wife! You see, one Sunday morning years ago, a gorgeous woman walked through the doors of the church. I was standing next to my brother in the lobby as she walked in, and she took my breath away. I can still tell you exactly what she was wearing. I grabbed my brother's arm, pulling him close to me, and said, "See that woman who just walked in? I'm going to marry her!"

My brother knew her, so I quickly got myself introduced to her, and I began to pursue a relationship. Over the course of time she and I became friends, and we fell in love. I married that beautiful woman. I had *a strong desire to acquire something that wasn't mine.* Ultimately, God gave her to me, and she agreed to be my wife.

If we're honest, we'll admit that this is how all love relationships usually work. We call it attraction. We see someone we "desire to acquire" and we begin to pursue the relationship. I've never met a man or woman who married a person he or she considered ugly. I am also not implying that beauty is only physical. The point is that attraction does involve physical desire, which leads to acquiring a mate. It's a legitimate desire for any unmarried person. If a married person entertained the same kinds of sexual-attraction thoughts, he or she would be guilty of adultery, according to Jesus' redefined standards.

Bible scholars have often agreed that Jesus wasn't talking about strong sexual attractions or sexual thoughts. He chose his words carefully. He has identified lust as a *perversion* of strong sexual desire. How? He distinguishes the woman in this passage as a married woman, using the Greek word *gyne*, which often means "wife." He is also speaking directly to married men. His choice of the word "adultery" indicates that this desire to acquire, among or directed toward married people, is equal to adultery.[3] Bible scholars agree that Jesus is not talking about the natural sexual drives of a single person seeking a mate. This makes the issue of lust much more defined for married people while it stays more ambiguous for the single person.

To give the impression that strong sexual urges and desires are always lust is irresponsible. Lust is a difficult thing to define—and we're going to delve deeply into the issue in our next chapter. For now, let it suffice to say that there is no universal standard to describe what lust is. Making lust synonymous to masturbation—because as many have said, "You can't do that without lusting"—is to superimpose a personal standard on all guys. Yet the Holy Spirit alone is responsible to convict our hearts regarding lust. One man's lust may not be lust for others. When someone tells me that "you can't masturbate without lust," I often ask if this is a personal confession. I clarify by asking, "Do you mean that *you*, personally, can't masturbate without lust?" If this is true, and there is personal conviction about lust and its association to masturbation, then it is sin for that person.

LICENSE, LEGALISM . . . OR NEITHER?

I once spoke to a number of guys attending a campus ministries group at a large state university. A small group of vocal and sincerely God-honoring guys had difficulty seeing that lust-and-masturbation is not a universal sin issue. Over and over, they claimed that the thinking and desires accompanying masturbation are clearly lust. After they debated their case for a while, I introduced another point of view.

I proposed that we agree, for the sake of argument, that masturbation and lust were "bedfellows," so to speak. I then asked, "Is masturbation the *beginning* or *end* of lust?"

If we're honest we'd have to agree that the sexual thoughts, desires, arousal, and even lust *precede* the need to masturbate. Once orgasm occurs, all of that is gone. Masturbation is the end of lust, not the beginning of lust. Masturbation isn't lust nor does it feed lust. It ends lustful episodes. I continued to explain that there are many godly men and women who believe that because masturbation follows the lust and shuts down the process, it becomes the way out that many people pray for. For these people, this deliverance from lust makes masturbation a gift from God.

They also see masturbation as God's design for delivering single believers from falling into deep sexual sin. Additionally, masturbation, as a gift from God, can keep married partners faithful to each other when they're separated. Couldn't this also be a "way of escape" that Paul talked about in 1 Corinthians 10:13? The context of the passage deals with questionable, or "gray," issues, for which no universal command or guideline applies. Paul said:

> *No temptation has overtaken you but such as is common to man; and God is faithful, who will not allow you to be tempted beyond what you are able, but with the temptation will provide the way of escape also, so that you will be able to endure it.*
> (NASB)

Those who hold to the "gift of God" view are quick to say that the issue of lust and its relation to masturbation can be included in this passage. Therefore this passage would mean there is universal *freedom* for everyone. They would say that masturbation is universally right. This is putting unfettered license on a gray issue and is equally as irresponsible as using the passage to say that masturbation is always sin.

The issue of masturbation cannot be regulated either by license ("anything goes") or by legalism ("nothing allowed"). No so-called proof texts in the Bible indicate that masturbation is wrong. No proof texts apply universal freedom to the issue, either. This would indicate that masturbation is going to be *a matter of personal conviction*. For some it will be sin. For others it won't.

But we still need to clear up some big questions about lust, right? That will be the goal of our next chapter.

THINK ABOUT IT!

1. Do you agree that the story of Onan is not about masturbation? Spend some time thinking through your reasons.

2. Why would the Old Testament citizens be so concerned about emissions and cleanliness? What are some theological implications?

3. Summarize, in your own words, the apostle Paul's views on marriage and singleness.

4. Do you believe that masturbation is always a matter of lust? Why or why not?

5. Consider what it means to avoid both license and legalism. Where are you in relation to these two poles of behavior? What would you like to change about your life in this regard?

I THINK, THEREFORE I'M . . . LUSTING?

For most teenage guys, getting "fired up" can occur when the wind shifts.

-----Original Message-----
From: Jeff [*jeffyscholar3@free2bfree.biz*]
Sent: Monday, April 11, 2002 2:42 PM
To: *sgerali@TH1NK.com*
Subject: Hi, from a former student . . .

Hey, Doc: Thanx for thinking about me. Life is going pretty good. Amy and I are trying to get stuff together for our upcoming wedding this June after graduation. We have a lot of decisions to make — one has to do with new jobs for both of us!

I'm struggling on another front, however. It's lust. I don't look at pornography, but I just can't seem to defeat this masturbation thing. I know it's probably weird for me to come right out and talk about this. But other than Jesus, who can I talk to that won't look at me funny or be weirded out by me bringing it up? (At least if you're weirded out, you're about a thousand miles away!)

Anyhow, this is just so frustrating. Some days, and even weeks, I'm just fine, and when temptation comes I simply think about more important things, like my walk with Jesus or my future wife. Then it's no problem. Other times it seems my body reacts before there's even time for my mind to engage.

I just want to walk in victory in this area of my life. I want the fruit of the Spirit: self-control. I've asked for it, and at times seem to have it, but where is the consistency? It is so defeating! I hate thinking these sexual things. I sometimes feel like God is abandoning me.

I'm open to prayer, advice, or whatever you have to offer from the Lord. Doc, if anything, I'm so glad that I was able to finally tell somebody. I love Jesus and hate it when I do something that isn't offering him my best. To be honest, right now I am frustrated to tears. And I want to resolve this before I get married this summer. Please tell me there is victory over this!—Jeff

Can you relate to Jeff's struggle? Over and over I hear guys say that they keep giving this sin to the Lord and yet he doesn't take it away. Satan seizes this struggle and begins the downward spiral of guilt, shame, and doubt.

Lust does hinder our relationship with God. It can engage us in an all-consuming battle that we come to believe is a hopeless struggle. I've experienced this myself, and the story is always the same: men broken and crying out to God for deliverance.

My answer to Jeff was, "Yes. There is victory for every man!" In order to gain victory, though, we need to allow God to realign our thinking. We can start by confronting our ideas of what lust is—or, more to the point, what lust is not.

DEFINING LUST . . . OR NOT

Defining lust is like trying to nail Jell-O to the wall—it just isn't going to happen. "Lust" is usually used in Scripture to mean a *strong desire* that is *sinful*. On the one hand, we're lead to believe that certain strong desires are inherently evil. On the other hand, we know that some strong desires are morally right. These desires, good or evil, are never universally defined. So what can we say about desire? Consider three basic points:

1. *Desire is as unique to each individual as a fingerprint.* Evil desires, or lusts, are personally unique. Some things that I desire will never hold an attraction for someone else. I desire to travel overseas; some of my friends never wish to leave the United States. If desires were universal we would all want travel or all want *not* to travel, depending upon the way God had wired up all human beings. But God didn't wire us with the same desires; he created each of us unique and thus gives us choices. Desire comes packaged individualized, not standardized.

2. *Intensity of desire must figure into the equation.* I can desire a Corvette and not be sinning. But given a different set of circumstances and internal weaknesses, that same desire can become evil. We soon come to the conclusion that "strong" desire is relative. Strong to one person may not be strong to the next, however. An individual may be susceptible to the slightest desire and, to him or her, it would be strong (and maybe even sinful). But to another individual it may not be strong.

Consider the person who struggles with gluttony, for example. The slightest exposure to, or thought of, food may constitute a strong desire to that person, whereas a person who isn't as susceptible to gluttony may have stronger desires, and eat a lot, and still not sin. The opposite of this may also be true. An individual can become calloused to strong desires and thus minimize the moral implications.

How often have you said, "I'm starving"? If we compare our raging appetite at suppertime with the need of a person who *really is* nutritionally wasting away, our desire for food could be interpreted as a sinful act of gluttony. The majority of the world eats less in a week than most Americans eat in a day. Would we interpret our American desires to satisfy our hunger as a lust for food? Have we become calloused, or is the intensity of that desire relative?

3. *The lust-boundaries have flexibility.* Suddenly we find ourselves wrestling with the complexity of issues surrounding desires, sinful or honorable. We see that it's not very easy, nor is it wise, to make any desire universal and then ascribe a weight of morality to that desire. Desires can be sinful. Lust is a sinful desire, but each person must be sensitive to the Holy Spirit's leading as to where the line is.

For the moment, let's stay with the food metaphor. Let's assume that gluttony is a personal issue and that I struggle with thoughts and desires about food. It would be foolish for me to think that because I lust for food *I should eliminate all thinking about food!* Wisdom would mandate that I control my thinking by gaining an understanding as to when those thoughts cross the boundary and become sinful for me. I like the way C. S. Lewis used the food analogy:

> You can get a large audience together for a strip-tease act —
> that is, to watch a girl undress on the stage. Now suppose you
> came to a country where you could fill a theatre by simply
> bringing a covered plate on to the stage and then slowly lifting
> the cover so as to let everyone see, just before the lights went out,

that it contained a mutton chop or a bit of bacon. Would you not think that in that country something had gone wrong with the appetite for food?

And would not anyone who had grown up in a different world think there was something equally [strange] about the state of the sex instinct among us?'

Lewis was talking about a "sex instinct" that had become tied to pornography, commercialism, and sensationalism. That's when desire can become sinful.

In order to get control over sinful lust, we must start by defining what lust *may not* be. I've chosen my words carefully, because we can't say that certain things are *not* lust. If we can't make universal claims on what a sinful desire *is*, then we can't make universal claims on what a sinful desire *isn't*.

"All sexual thoughts are impure because I can't think of a pure sexual thought. Sexual thoughts just pop into your head when you don't want them to; you just have to live with it. I try to think about other things to get it off my mind."   **— Jarred, 15**

A good general definition of lust comes from writer Frederick Buechner: "Lust is the craving for salt of a person who is dying of thirst."[2] But that definition's generalizing quality still leaves us with a challenge: We still can't say, cut and dried, that some *specific thing* is or is not lust. So let's look at four things that aren't necessarily lust. In other words it's a *possibility* for each of these "to be or not to be" lust.

POSSIBILITY #1: THINKING SEXUAL THOUGHTS

God created us as sexual beings. He also created sex as something good, with a double purpose of procreation and pleasure. God created sex good. Let me say it again: *God created sex good!* Because of this basic truth, we know we'll think sexual thoughts because we were created as sexual beings and because sex was created for our pleasure. It is good.

Many have tried to define sexual *lust* as being sexual *thinking*—that thinking sexual thoughts, or thinking too much about sexual things, is lust. Others say that thinking sexual thoughts isn't lust, but having an *obsession* with sexual thinking is lust. I would agree that an obsession of any kind would border on sin. The Bible teaches us about a balanced and controlled life and that we shouldn't be mastered by anything (see 1 Corinthians 6:12). Yet the basic question here is, How much is too much? considering that it is in our created design to think sexually. Too much for one person may not be too much for another.

From the time I began writing this book until finishing the manuscript, I contemplated, talked about, researched, wrestled with, and even at times subconsciously dealt with thoughts about masturbation and sexuality. I probably thought about this more over those last few months than I had during my entire life so far. I even talked with God about this topic of masturbation more than ever. I asked him to guide and guard my words and shape them into thoughts—sexual thoughts—that pleased him.

Some could say that what I just described was an *obsession*. Is it? To quantify a person's thought life would be ridiculous. It would be foolish to say that a person may only think of seven sexual thoughts or have five sexual desires per day because that is the norm. After he or she has filled the minimum daily "sexual thought" requirement, then he or she has entered into the "obsession zone." Every thought and desire beyond the supposed norm would then be lustful sin.

Okay, it's ridiculous to set a number on sexual thoughts. But some still believe that obsession can be quantified. They believe they are the judges of how much is too much; therefore, they elevate their opinions to the level of Scripture and their convictions to equality with the authority of the Holy Spirit. Obsession is something that the Holy Spirit regulates individually. He convicts each of us differently according to the ways that he is changing and perfecting us. Lust does involve sexual thinking, sometimes a lot of sexual thinking. *But sexual thinking, and lots of it, may not always be lust.*

I was talking about this to a friend.

"I understand what you're saying, Steve," he said. "But I have a hard time with it because the Bible says we're to think about 'pure' things."

"Agreed!" I responded. "And I assume you're referring to Philippians 4:8, which says 'whatever is pure, whatever is lovely, whatever is of good repute, if there is any excellence and if anything worthy of praise, dwell on these things' (NASB). But where did you get the idea that sexual thinking isn't pure?"

He looked at me with a confused stare. "I guess I just assumed it."

"But look, God created us sexual, and he created us good. Thinking sexual thoughts originates out of his sexual design for us. Therefore they can be true, honorable, right, lovely, of good repute, excellent, praiseworthy, and even pure."

Do you agree? I'm simply saying that to see God's creative design as anything less than good—and to lump all sexual thinking into the category of lust—is not true, good, right, or pure, and therefore, not excellent for my mind to dwell on.

POSSIBILITY #2: HAVING A SEX DRIVE

Remember Jeff's e-mail at the beginning of this chapter? He spoke of times when his body reacts even before his mind has a chance to kick into gear. Jeff was talking about strong sexual urges, or what many would call a "sex drive." These sexual urges are, in fact, God-instilled. Remember that God designed sex for our pleasure and therefore instills strong long-ings, urges, or drives in us to allow us to pursue that which he created for us. These are triggered by *external* and *internal* factors. Many times those drives are hormonally induced, which is the internal factor.

Don't discount the internal igniters! At certain times people, both male and female, are more sexually driven than at other times. Our primary sex organ is the brain, and our brain regulates hormones in our body to keep us healthy. Those hormones are called *androgens* and are responsi-ble for reproductive and physiological growth during puberty and ado-lescence. They also regulate the reproductive system throughout life (such as sperm and semen production in males and menstruation in females) and are responsible for "turning us on" sexually.

There will be times throughout a man's life when his body will be producing larger amounts of sperm and semen than at other times. The hormones responsible for that production also induce sexual thoughts and drive. A man may find his sexual urges so strong that "his body reacts before his mind engages," to put it in Jeff's terms.

The same is true of a woman's body. Right before a woman ovu-lates, her body will produce higher levels of androgens, making her reproductive system work. These androgens also produce sexual appetite, and she finds herself more sexually driven than at other times.

As a teen, I heard a youth speaker talk about "fleeing youthful lust." His definition of youthful lust was anything that led to sexual arousal. But sex drives are often arousing. Arousal is normal and good, but this well-meaning speaker didn't think so. He didn't know about androgens and their effect on the human body. He kept saying that we should avoid anything that would "fire us up" sexually. For most teenage guys, getting "fired up" can occur when the wind shifts.

Now, I would agree that we should avoid certain things, and we'll get to that in a moment when we talk about external factors that trigger the sex drive. But there are times when a person's sexual appetite will be greater than at other times, and external factors will not play a dominant role.

Throughout high school and college, I felt ashamed, guilty, and vile every time I had strong sexual drives. I would literally weep before God, asking him to take these lustful feelings and thoughts away. He didn't, because my body needed them for its growth and development. I was growing according to his perfect plan, and now I wish someone had told me that those thoughts were triggered by the hormones pumping through my system. I wish someone had freed me from the burden caused by the lie I'd believed—that all sexual drive and sexual arousal was youthful lust.

Be careful with those external exciters! External factors also cause sex drive and arousal. We live in a sex-saturated society. Every day we're bombarded with sexual messages and images. And many of those messages need to be avoided. Second Timothy 2:22 (NASB) says, "Flee from youthful lusts and pursue righteousness, faith, love and peace, with those who call on the Lord from a pure heart."

For a young, single guy, seeing a beautiful woman or engaging in a conversation with a woman can be arousing. Even holding hands can be arousing. These external factors trigger androgens that give way to a type of arousal that's essential in mate selection. Arousal triggered by external factors may not always be youthful lust.

Does this mean that the arousal *could* be youthful lust?

Yes.

The amount of time, intensity, and priority I give to external factors that create arousal could make those arousing thoughts sinful lusts for me. Again, it's critical to depend on the Holy Spirit to discern when we're crossing the line.

It's also important to note that not all arousal by external factors is subjective. Looking at pornographic materials, having cyber-sex on the Internet, dialing up phone-sex numbers, and entertaining inappropriate sexual thoughts (like having sex with children), among other things, cross the line. Many of these things are even viewed as morally wrong by a godless society. Involvement in them can create a ferocious sexual appetite and can lead to sexual addiction. Masturbation then reinforces the deviance produced by this type of arousal.

The important thing here is trusting Christ to be Lord over our sexuality. He must be in control of creating the balance that allows us to experience healthy, God-given sexual urges and arousal rather than inappropriate, deceptive sexual drives.

POSSIBILITY #3: DEVELOPING YOUR SEXUAL "MAP"

During one of my college Human Sexuality courses, I asked students to think about, and write down, what physically attracted them to the opposite sex. After a few minutes I called on a few people who I knew would be secure enough to share.

One guy said, "Hair."

Another said, "Breasts."

One girl said, "Abs."

Another said, "Eyes."

It soon became apparent that each person in the room was attracted to different things. As we continued the discussion and started talking about sexual turn-ons, the responses were similarly diverse. People didn't have the same sexual desires; each had different sexual tastes.

How is it that some people are more attracted to blondes and others to brunettes? Why are some guys "leg men" and others "breast men"? Why are some women turned on by a man's shoulders and others by his backside?

"I was led to believe that your view of women would be distorted if you masturbated, because masturbation was on the same level as porn."   **—Brian, 22**

Attraction doesn't stop with the physical, either. After an initial physical attraction, we're drawn deeper by personality, values, passions, and a host of other attraction variables. So why aren't we all attracted to the same things? Clearly, God allows us to develop sexual tastes. He allows individual tastes and desires to create a unique sexual template within each of our lives. This sexual template is called *sexual mapping* or *sexual patterning.*

Sexual mapping involves a number of things, beginning at conception. I alluded to the fact that some people have more of a sex drive (or *libido*) than others. Testosterone directly affects sex drive in both men and women. A strong libido can result from higher amounts of testosterone in someone's system. This, in turn, can be affected by something known as an *androgen wash,* which occurs during the growth of the fetus. Sexual mapping does have a physiological component to it.

Our drives, tastes, and desires regarding the opposite sex, sexual instincts, gender roles, affection, dreams, romance, and even negative sexual trauma can affect our patterning. Sexual mapping can be shaped and reinforced by the emotions created by a love song, the smell of a particular perfume, a tender, romantic touch, or even masturbation.

Much of our sexual mapping results from learning. Sexuality, while it's somewhat instinctual, is also a learned thing. That's why we can keep getting better at sex with practice. God created us to be sexual throughout our lives. So he allows us to grow—sexually. That is part of the sexual pattern he builds into us. To try to avoid sexual curiosities or strong likes runs counter to how God wired us. These things may play a role in lust but, in and of themselves, may not be lust.

Learning and acquiring individual sexual tastes largely happens through our senses. It is *sensual.* Sounds and smells can get us sexually charged, thus we spend hundreds of dollars on love songs and perfumes. Taste can get us sexually charged, and certain foods have aphrodisiacal effects on certain individuals. Touch is also a turn-on. Anything from holding hands to intercourse becomes a sensual, sexual experience. Junior highers learn these turn-ons by hitting or roughhousing with members of the opposite sex. That is a sensual experience. Such sensual excitement is shaping the sexual patterning.

In Western culture we're largely influenced by sight. We see things that we find pleasant, beautiful, and attractive. We start to gravitate toward those things and search for those things. Because "beauty is in the eye of the beholder," it's left to individual tastes. Thus sexual attraction is the result of seeing first. I have never met any people who say they searched for the ugliest person they could find to marry; everyone marries someone he or she considers to be a beautiful partner. For the most part, there's an initial attraction by sight that starts the pursuit of a relationship. That's good!

The reason sight is such a dominating sexual sense in the West is because we're an *iconic* culture. We've conditioned ourselves to learn and pattern our tastes by using pictures, or icons. We even create "mental pictures." For example, think of a delicious hamburger and see what leaps into your mind . . .

> *a luscious sesame-seed bun . . .*
> *a juicy meal patty . . .*
> *yellow cheese, white onion, rich, ripe tomato . . .*
> *crisp green lettuce and pickles . . .*
> *red catsup . . .*
> *yellow mustard . . .*
> *pure white mayo . . .*

Is your mouth starting to water? You can almost smell it, right? Keep it up and you'll be running to Mickey D's.

But when you get your burger it doesn't look like the picture you had in your mind—or even the picture plastered to the restaurant window. You eat it, nonetheless, with great enjoyment. You are iconic, influenced and conditioned by icons. You balance your expectations

because you are also a realist and understand that you've been motivated by . . . just a picture.

"I think God made us to think about sexual things, but it becomes lust when you personalize it."   —Rick, 16

The development of sexual tastes is equally iconic. We see beauty
flashed in front of us in every advertisement. An advertisement doesn't
even have to be sexual for us to start forming our sexual tastes based on
the beauty we see in the icons (people) who represent products. We
start to form ideals about the person who turns us on sexually. We begin
to pursue people who fit into the picture we form. That's why some are
attracted to blondes, brunettes, hair, eyes, and so on. Many of those
mental pictures are represented by the celebrities we see. We commonly say that those people have "sex appeal," and we don't consider
sex appeal to be wrong.

I was talking to a group of men about lust and masturbation, when one
guy spoke up. "I think masturbation is all right if you think about a face-
less person," he said. Many hold to this view. I personally don't know if
that is possible to do, because I couldn't do it, but my experience doesn't
mean that it's universal to all men. He said this because he believed producing a picture of someone in his mind took him across the lust
boundary. When masturbating, we might generate thoughts of celebrities
or people we're attracted to. We create a mental picture. We are iconic.
Can this reduce someone to an object? Yes. Does it always? No.

Can this go south fast? Yep! Like everything good and right, Satan
can twist it to become something evil. We need to guard our heart and
mind. The way we do that is to understand that we are iconic. There is
nothing wrong with that. It goes south when we begin to idealistically
objectify things, condition ourselves to perfection, and keep feeding

our mind false, unrealistic images. This is one of the major deceptions the porn industry sells. The reason we don't have a difficult time with the burger is because we are realistic. The same applies to sex. Realism creates the check-and-balance against iconic idealism and vice versa. The combination helps to keep us growing.

Deeper issues can come into play, leading someone to *devalue* people who they see as the objects of their tastes. But objectification can also be a good thing. An object can become something to be admired and valued as easily as it can be devalued. People can be the objects of our respect, affection, love, and honor. An icon is simply the broader representation of the desires and tastes that we form.

At this point you may be thinking, *Okay, Steve. Let's slow down here. So where's the difference between a mental picture in my mind and a pornographic picture in front of me?*

Once again, the issue here is not objectification as much as it is the values, attitudes, and motives conjured by the picture. The art community has wrestled with this for centuries. Where is the boundary line between the pornographic and the purely artistic?

We would all agree there's a difference between the nudity portrayed in Michelangelo's Sistine Chapel ceiling and the nudity in *Playboy*. We also know that a *National Geographic* magazine photo depicting nude natives may not be immoral, but it can accomplish the same sexual response as porn. The conflict lies in the heart and mind of the beholder. The Bible tells us that the heart is deceitful and desperately wicked (see Jeremiah 17:9). Once again, sensitivity to the Holy Spirit's conviction is critical. But saying that we should avoid all things sensuous is denying God's creative sexual design and leads to a bondage equal to that created by porn.

Sexual fantasy, as well as sexual mapping, also plays out in a wet dream. There's very little controversy or question here. Many who believe masturbation is sin because of the fantasy, imagery, and desire that accompany it quickly backpedal on the issue of wet dreams. They logically deduce that wet dreams have no moral significance or consequence because they occur while a person is semiconscious. If the guy isn't consciously controlling this process, then he's off the hook.

They fail to see that dreams are also the result of the data that we take into our brain consciously. They fail to see that during a wet dream the brain is downloading data that has been stored there through sensory intake, or sexual mapping. The guy who's having this dream is playing out his desires about a beautiful partner designed by his sexual tastes. She may even have a face, be a person he's attracted to, or be a celebrity icon. He then instinctually fantasizes a sexual encounter and sex play. This ends up in full orgasmic bliss. But this is now acceptable because he presumably did not control it? That seems to be a double standard.

As a matter of fact, more of a pro-masturbation argument could be made because the masturbator *does* control it and is not allowing his dreams to be master over him (see 1 Corinthians 6:12). It's interesting to note that the world of Tissot, Graham, and Kellogg couldn't account for nocturnal emissions either. Their semen-conservation theories broke down at this point. Many of those anti-masturbatory advocates believed that wet dreams were devil-produced and therefore God eliminated the effects of that sin on the person's life. Others believed that because the victim couldn't control the wet dream, his ejaculation was different and had less of an effect on the nervous system and overall health. Despite this, they still created devices that, if worn at night, would supposedly keep men from having wet dreams.

Satan still uses the same double-standard tactics today that he did in the past. Either we level the playing field and call all sexual fantasy and thought leading to orgasm sin, or we loosen our belt and become more intelligent and embracing about psychosexual (mind and sex) processes.

POSSIBILITY #4: REHEARSING FOR REALITY WITH FANTASY

Immediately, the words *sexual fantasy* conjure visions of orgies, lewd sexual encounters, and a host of sordid images. The adult sex industry has capitalized on the word and has even twisted its true meaning. All that is involved in the porn industry is wicked. But we must not allow good sexual responses to be lumped in with it. Christians must stand against false teachings that would make us repress what God has designed as good.

Often lust is made synonymous with sexual fantasy. Then masturbation is called wrong because "you can't do it without fantasy." The line of logic deduces that if fantasy is lust, and you can't masturbate without fantasy, then it follows that you can't therefore masturbate without lusting. However, like any other forms of sexual thinking, fantasy must first be clearly defined. We might then conclude that there are elements in sexual fantasy that are God-designed.

Lets begin by talking about fantasy without it being sexual. Children get together and play. They fantasize about being firemen, princesses, doctors, mommies or daddies, cowboys, cops, dancers, nurses, and so on. Often they play games that spring from their fantasies. They rehearse their imagined roles, and their play prepares them for their futures. I wanted to be a pastor from the time I was seven years old. I remember playing church with my friends and I'd be the preacher. I even took offerings (not really—my mom wouldn't let me keep any money). That type of child play is rehearsal, a normal part of growing up.

If we didn't use that dirty word *fantasy* and spoke, instead, of sexual *rehearsal*, we might begin to see the process differently. Fantasy involves a strong element of rehearsal. We rehearse being sexual. While sex is learned, it also has aspects that are instinctual. For example, when persons mature sexually, they *instinctually* know the how-to's of intercourse without being coached through the process. But they *learn*, over time, how to make intercourse more pleasurable and meaningful.

Part of what comes to us instinctually is the ability to create sexual rehearsal. Everyone daydreams about his or her honeymoon night, for example. We rehearse passionate kisses in our mind. We think about sex play that involves romantic interludes, exotic settings, even some element of adventure. We may rehearse in our mind those sex roles and actions with people who we view as potential partners. In his e-mail, Jeff is consumed with an upcoming wedding. He imagines his fiancée as his wife. He rehearses their honeymoon night in his mind. This will allow him to be confident, to be loving, to be romantic, to maximize his and her pleasure.

Of course, sexual rehearsal could also create anxiety about a honeymoon night. It can give rise to fears, questions, and nerves. Think about it: A person wouldn't be nervous about sex if he or she didn't go through some form of sexual rehearsal. The rehearsal conjures up ideas of inadequacy or insecurity and then nervousness. Regardless, sexual rehearsal is a natural part of being wired up "sexually good."

Somehow we've gotten the idea that thinking through sexual situations, daydreaming of sex with a spouse some day, or envisioning passionate sexual circumstances is all lustful thinking. While it could be, it is not always lust. It could be normal, God-instilled sexual rehearsal.

Even God's Word gives us examples of this. Song of Solomon conveys passionate, erotic sexual situations for us. The Shulammite woman in this play says, "All night long on my bed I looked for the one my heart loves; I looked for him but did not find him" (3:1). She is waiting, longing, daydreaming, rehearsing. Read the rest of the chapter and you'll see that she even goes out to find him.

"I thought thinking about sexual things was wrong. That made all sexual thoughts wrong, including masturbation."
—Jake, 20

Sexual rehearsal involves planning out, and planning for, sex. I have often said that I would love to see someone translate the book of Song of Solomon in the vernacular of the day. It would be extremely arousing. It creates clear mental pictures and generates a healthy, God-honoring form of sexual rehearsal. Clearly our sexuality and spirituality share some common bonds. Here is how one writer put it:

> *The man's daydreaming is the urgent religious searching of the mystic wanting to be wholly one—with the fount of life. It is honorable, honest, and healthy yearning, and our daydreamer is neither the first nor the last to suppose that fount comes in the form of a woman—a nurturing, responsive woman.*[3]

Besides the element of rehearsal, sexual fantasy also contains another good aspect: *sexual imagination.* This is a close parallel to sexual rehearsal and it's often hard to tell them apart. But again, we often get the impression that lust is the same as sexual imagination. Yet it's hard to understand sex at all without imagining it. Many people say that they learned about sex from their friends. When I probe a bit, I come to the conclusion that they put things together from conversations and then figured it out. We have the ability to do this because we are created with a strong sexual imagination.

Sexual imagination keeps sex in marriages from becoming mechanical and boring. Partners imagine sexual situations and then have the freedom to act on their imaginations. They may even have rehearsed that situation in their minds prior to the encounter.

We can't even learn sexual morals and biblical sexual principles without having sexual imagination. Many young men and women have abstained from any sexual contact in their relationships. They may have chosen this because they formulated a conviction about sex from God's Word. But before a person can formulate conviction, he or she must imagine the thing to which the conviction speaks!

For example, Solomon reminded the young man in Proverbs to let the breasts of his wife satisfy him at all times and that he should be always exhilarated with his partner's love (see Proverbs 5:18-19). The point is fidelity in marriage. The writer isn't mandating action to married men; he is telling all men to enjoy the bodies and love of their wives. Unmarried men can only imagine. It would be pointless for God to say this to youth if they *couldn't* imagine. In other words, the sexual imagination that keeps marriages growing and healthy doesn't begin when a person gets married. It is part of being sexual through one's life span.

"But Steve, those passages speak about sex with a wife!" you might say. "So rehearsal and imagination are acceptable if we are thinking about a spouse."

Well, this is true. But those passages aren't *exclusive* to married people. I've heard people confront unmarried men and women, saying that they should eliminate those thoughts because they aren't thinking about their spouses. Well, of course they aren't, because they can't know who their spouses are yet! Are we supposed to expect that unmarried people be nonsexual beings? No, because sexual rehearsal and imagination must take place throughout one's life span, preparing us for and perpetuating good sex. Scripture never implies that sexuality begins at marriage.

Naturally, sexual imagination and rehearsal have different consequences and outcomes for married persons and single persons. If a married person rehearses and imagines sexual scenes with someone other than his or her spouse, then it is adulterous lust (see Matthew 5:27-28).

I THINK, THEREFORE . . . I'M NORMAL

As we've seen, sexual thinking is a part of being sexual for all of us. We are created with the ability to acquire, shape, and cultivate our own sexual tastes. Our mind will create sexual ideas and images for us. We will imagine, dream, and rehearse sexual situations.

This is not wrong. It is God-designed.

And, as I have said throughout this chapter, there is a fine line between God-given sexuality and sinful lust. Lust can and often does involve our created sex drive. But sexual thinking, urges, desires, sexual patterning, and even sexual rehearsal and imagination are part of how God designed sexuality to be good. It seems we rarely talk about those things in a positive light. Rather, we give the impression that they are always wrong and should always be avoided.

We even cringe when we hear phrases like "sexual urges" and "sexual fantasy." Sadly, we have reduced a God-given gift to something repressed and dark. We have given ground to Satan by letting him deceive us into thinking all of our sexual impulses are lustful. Then Satan makes lust, or a counterfeit of lust, the focus of our thinking. It becomes all-consuming, self-absorbing, and defeating. Instead of focusing on the Lord of our sexuality, we channel all of our energy in working to eliminate something that we can't eliminate. This only puts us in a position to be defeated, shamed, and burdened.

I met a woman once who said, "I believe that every thought about sex is lustful until you get married. I also don't think I need to learn about sex, because God makes that happen naturally when you get married." This young lady feared thinking sexual things and expended great amounts of energy keeping herself from sexual thoughts. When she finally did marry, she was in such anxiety over this that she felt dirty every time her husband made love to her.

But there is freedom in Christ. He has redeemed us from sexual repression. Yes, we need to run from lust, but not by running into the arms of another deception that keeps us shamefully burdened.

The bottom line: Masturbation doesn't always involve lust. Lust can occur with or without masturbation. Masturbation, for some, can be a freeing control and release over God-given hormonally induced sexual urges. For others it can be a way of escape from a lust that could give way to great sexual sin. Still another may be prompted by the Holy Spirit to avoid masturbation entirely because of the work that God is doing to refine that individual's life. If this is true, conviction provides liberation but not shame. For all, there is freedom from sexual shame.

On the other hand, if you are struggling with certain desires and/or behaviors that could legitimately be labeled sinful lust, then I want to leave you with some hopeful words: God calls you to look to him for the comfort, strength, and perseverance you need to keep growing in him. Give yourself and your struggles to him, day by day, and he will carry you through. I especially like how C. S. Lewis once put it in *Mere Christianity*. I'll leave you with his eloquent words of encouragement.

> *We may, indeed, be sure that perfect chastity—like perfect charity—will not be attained by any merely human efforts. You must ask for God's help. Even when you have done so, it may seem to you for a long time that no help, or less help than you need, is being given. Never mind. After each failure, ask forgiveness, pick yourself up, and try again.*
>
> *Very often what God first helps us toward is not the virtue itself but just this power of always trying again. For however important chastity (or courage, or truthfulness, or any other virtue) may be, this process trains us in habits of the soul which are more important still. It cures our illusions about ourselves and teaches us to depend on God. We learn, on the one hand, that we cannot trust ourselves even in our best moments, and, on the other, that we need not despair even in our worst, for our failures are forgiven. The only fatal thing is to sit down content with anything less than perfection.[4]*

THINK ABOUT IT!

1. What is your personal definition of *lust?* How has your definition been influenced by the discussion in this chapter?

2. Have you ever believed that thinking sexual thoughts is always wrong? What have you learned from the author about this?

3. List some of the items on your particular sexual map. How are you like or unlike some of your friends when it comes to what attracts you or turns you on?

4. Describe some of the ways that sexual fantasy may be okay for a Christian.

5. Respond to the closing quote by C. S. Lewis. Where does it ring a bell with you? How might you say it differently?

CHAPTER SEVEN

IN THE GRAY ZONE: A WISDOM ISSUE

I'm paying five dollars into the college's building fund for every time I do it. Hey, if I keep going at this rate, they'll probably name a whole dorm after me.

My scholarly English friend turned to me and said, "Steve, it's clearly a middle issue."

A *what?* I thought maybe our American and British languages had failed to make contact, so I pressed further.

"Right, Steve. You see, I think masturbation would be a difficult subject to write about because there seem to be only two sides. Either you believe it's acceptable or you believe it's not. Yet when it comes to those kinds of issues, I learned an important lesson from a wise and godly teacher. He stated that there is *always* a 'middle.' God is just as much Lord over the middle as he is Lord over the left and the right."

As we stood there in the great hall of Mansfield College, University of Oxford, my friend recounted the biblical story as his teacher had so often interpreted it:

> *When Jesus made his entry into Jerusalem, the Jews of the day, who embraced him as Messiah, believed he was entering the city to establish his kingdom. To them, there were only two options: either he entered militarily to overthrow the Roman government (as the Zealots believed) or he entered politically and embraced*

the Romans, incorporating their ideologies and his influential leadership to gain a stronghold for a new government (as the Herodians believed).

Instead, Jesus rides in humbly, on a donkey, not embracing the Romans nor waging war against them. Not militantly with great power, nor politically with great influence. Jesus operated in the middle. He did that quite a bit.

It makes sense to me to see masturbation as a middle issue. But how do you see it?

We've talked about the Bible's essential silence on this issue. The result is that deciding about the rightness or wrongness of masturbation becomes *a matter of prayerful wisdom for each believer.*

The early church dealt with many things that Scripture did not directly address. One of those issues concerned meat that was sacrificed to idols. Here's how the controversy played out: The Hebrews believed there were certain practices required by God and written in the Law that kept a person in right relationship with God. If a person knew that there was some sin in his or her life, then that person would be required to make an offering of atonement. This would put him or her in right relationship with God as a forgiven child.

But what if there were some things that the person didn't know were sin? What if you felt like your relationship with God was not where it should be? Well, in this case you could make a *peace* offering. The priest would cut an animal in two equal parts. One part would be burned on the altar as an offering to God. Then you were required to take the other part home to cook and eat it. When you sat down to that meal you were actually having dinner with God, a ritual of commitment and alliance to him.

Here's where a big problem raised its ugly head: This same practice was used to symbolize commitment and fellowship with pagan gods! Eating meat sacrificed to an idol was an act of being bound to that god. Now, while the law was clear about the sacrifice, it wasn't clear about the issue of eating meat sacrificed to idols.

So Paul addressed this issue of eating meat as a *middle* issue or, more theologically, a wisdom issue. These cover matters where liberty or restraint may be applied. Some may have been free to exercise liberty here. They would say, "Relax, guys. All of us Christians know that idols are just silly old lumps of stone or wood, right? There's only one true God in heaven, so why waste good food? Eat and give thanks!"

Others would have been free to exercise restraint with their freedom. They would say, "Hey, I know those idols aren't real and the meat is okay. But for the sake of peace, and so as not to offend any other Christians, I'll just limit myself to other kinds of food."

For some the issue would have been clearly sin. They would say, "If a piece of meat has been dedicated to another god besides the Lord of the universe, then it's been tainted. How could I take something blessed by an enemy of the true God and pretend that it's just ordinary old food? No way!"

See how the issue of masturbation becomes a middle issue?

Let's be clear. Just because there is liberty for some, doesn't mean that there is total license or—God forbid—no boundaries. Paul wrote:

> *"Everything is permissible for me"*—*but not everything is* ben-eficial. *"Everything is permissible for me"*—*but I will not be mastered by anything.* (*1 Corinthians 6:12, emphasis added*)

> *"Everything is permissible"*—*but not everything is* construc-
> tive. (*1 Corinthians 10:23, emphasis added*)

Thankfully, Paul offered some guidelines that can help us make decisions about a wisdom issue. That is, he qualified the boundaries as to whether an activity is *beneficial, constructive,* or *mastering.* Let's unpack these three guidelines as they relate to masturbation.

PERMISSIBLE AND BENEFICIAL

Is masturbation beneficial? There's a lot of debate about this, but depending on your viewpoint, you may answer yes. We've already looked at three perspectives that could support a strong argument here. The *first* is that masturbation may be God's way of offering escape from greater sexual temptation and sin. As a way out, masturbation becomes beneficial.

The *second* perspective is that masturbation becomes the *end* of an episode of struggle with lust. Strong desires can keep the fires of sinful lust burning bright. Of course, others would argue that God can deliver us from lust without masturbation. This is true, and it's important to note that God can and does free us from lust apart from masturbation. But it's equally true that he can and does use masturbation as a means of relief for some individuals. We must rely on the Holy Spirit for conviction and discernment in this area.

The *third* perspective focuses on masturbation's ability to relieve certain physiological problems. We've already noted that masturbation helps those suffering from physical sexual dysfunction. It may also relieve the male sexual and physiological tension that builds up from the production of sperm and semen. While these potential benefits may not come into play for all people, they do for some. Those people would find some liberty with masturbation.

"Maybe masturbation can keep people from going too far. I know a lot of guys who get caught in sexual sins, and I wonder if masturbation would have kept them from getting into trouble." **—Rick, 16**

PERMISSIBLE AND CONSTRUCTIVE

Paul's second guideline is that "'Everything is permissible'—but not everything is constructive" (1 Corinthians 10:23). The word *constructive* may also be translated *edifying* (think of an edifice, a building). Paul said that while there is freedom in all things, those things may not build us up.

But how do we determine what builds us up and what doesn't? I propose that the issue of masturbation, right or wrong, has that potential to build up an individual because the struggle with it makes us continuously run to God and depend on him.

The writer of Hebrews told us to "fix our eyes on Jesus" (Hebrews 12:2). Paul reminded us to "press on toward the goal to win the prize for which God has called me heavenward in Christ Jesus" (Philippians 3:14). I think it would be fair to say that anytime I take my focus off of Christ I venture into a *non-edifying* pattern. The *struggle* over masturbation can divert my focus from Christ even more than the *act* of masturbation.

I've talked to countless men who've become so absorbed in the battle to eliminate masturbation from their lives that they have taken their focus off of God and put it on the struggle. Satan delights in this. Focusing on our fight keeps us living in defeat and shame—because human willpower always loses (and actually feeds the problem). This is not *building us up*. We have been deceived into thinking that godliness consists in the attempts we make to *eliminate* the sin in our lives. If we buy into this view of godliness, we focus on our sin rather than the Christ who has already eliminated our sin and makes us a new creation. Godliness is not our attempt to eliminate our sin; instead, godliness is all about *how we deal with the sin in our lives*. Do we keep going back to God's forgiveness, mercy, and grace?

I love the speech uttered by an old general in the movie *Babette's Feast*. He had suddenly been struck with just how free is God's infinite love and grace—free for the taking and enjoying. At the end of a surprising, sumptuous gift of a meal—a heavenly feast—he stands among new friends and says:

> *We have all of us been told that grace is to be found in the universe. But in our human foolishness and short-sightedness we imagine divine grace to be finite. For this reason we tremble. . . .*
>
> *We tremble before making our choice in life, and after having made it, again we tremble in fear of having chosen wrong. But the moment comes when our eyes are opened, and we see and realize that grace is infinite.*
>
> *Grace, my friends, demands nothing from us but that we shall await it with confidence, and* acknowledge it in gratitude. *Grace, brothers, makes no conditions and singles out none of us in particular; grace takes us all to its bosom and proclaims general amnesty.*[1] (emphasis added)

If you say masturbation is sin, you may have to conclude that this is one of the primary things that keeps you running to God. Good. He is the source of all grace, mercy, strength, and joy. You will find no condemnation there.

But find freedom to struggle.

Struggle hard.

Struggle often, and struggle without shame.

If it were not for the struggles in our lives, we would become self-sufficient and wouldn't need God. He allows us to run to him. He allows us to keep coming into his presence, where we find that his "lovingkindnesses indeed never cease, for His compassions never fail. They are new every morning" (Lamentations 3:22-23, NASB). He meets us at that very place where we struggle. *He* becomes the focal point, not the sin and struggle. He himself is the builder and edifier.

Remember that Paul wants us to ask whether this liberty is *not* constructive, as well. When Paul said, "Not everything is constructive," he wasn't saying that every liberty always has to be a constructive means to an end. He was saying that some things merit asking the question "Is this harmful to me?"

If everything we did had to be an edifying means to an end, then we'd have a difficult time explaining how drinking lemonade, riding a roller coaster, watching TV, driving a car, and doing countless other things edifies or builds us up. The simple truth is that these activities aren't destructive (they are not *non*-edifying, to use a double negative) and therefore may fall under the umbrella of liberty.

Does masturbation edify? Is masturbation destructive? There's no universal, definitive answer. Only the Holy Spirit holds the position and authority to legislate that answer in each person's life.

PERMISSIBLE BUT NOT MASTERING

Paul's third guideline is that "'everything is permissible for me'—but I will not be mastered by anything" (1 Corinthians 6:12). He realized the potential for *everything* to master us, even in areas of liberty. His advice, therefore, is that we keep everything in check.

Remember, we've said that habitual practices don't necessarily mean being mastered by those things. The solution to "not being mastered" is to exercise self-control. Ironically, eliminating a practice altogether may not mean that I'm getting it under control. People attempt to eliminate habits every day. Take smoking, for example. I've had friends who've struggled to eliminate it from their life. While they have to exercise control over their will, their intended purpose is to stop the habit, not control it.

One of my colleagues who teaches youth ministry at another college was telling me that a group of his male students decided they wouldn't be mastered by masturbation. They decided to hold each other accountable to control it. Many wanted to quit masturbating altogether, while others wanted to limit the frequency as a means of being in control. These guys decided they were going to pay five dollars into the college's building fund every time they masturbated.

One of the students was meeting with my colleague, and he seemed quite defeated. He wanted to talk about strategies to help him get things under control. When my friend asked him how he was doing with the five-dollar method, the student replied, "Hey, if I keep going at this rate, they'll probably name a whole dorm after me."

Many times we have unrealistic expectations about what it means to control something and not be mastered by it. For me, there are two ways to think about it:

1. *Get rid of it!* Not being mastered by something may indeed require its elimination. For example, if somebody has an alcohol problem, it would be ridiculous for him to say he's going to "cut back" on drinking.

I spoke to a youth pastor friend this week who had to be tough with one of his college students who has a severe drinking problem. The student thought he was getting things under control because he was only getting drunk once *every other* week instead of once a week!

The alcohol has control over him, so he needs to stop his drinking, rather than just control it, if he's going to be master over the substance. If masturbation is a sin that masters an individual, or if masturbation is used to reinforce an out-of-control sin like using pornography, then gaining control means getting rid of it.

2. *Control it and enjoy it!* Not being mastered by something may mean I control it but get pleasure from it as well. We can use the examples of eating desserts, or drinking coffee, or sleeping too much. I don't want these things to control me, so instead of participating excessively I limit or control my intake and practice. Eating sweets or drinking coffee may not be a sin for me. But they may be sin for someone else who's out of control with them. Although it isn't a sin issue for me, I am still required to be wise so as not to be mastered by anything.

Can't masturbation be the same? Many men have determined to be the master over it by planning and controlling the times and frequency. They've talked about the temptation to engage in masturbation recklessly, but they exercise self-control. This is similar to trying to stay in control over anything in our lives.

For example, I've coached college students who are undisciplined about their sleeping patterns. Many have decided they can sleep in on Saturdays, but the rest of the week they will stick to a set schedule, even though they might have opportunities to sleep in during the week. The entire issue here has to do with remaining disciplined. For some, masturbation may be all about discipline.

FREEDOM AND SELF-CONTROL

The Corinthians had a problem thinking that liberty was their license to engage in all kinds of sin, even sexual sin. Yes, Paul had taught that they were free. But just because they had a relationship with Christ didn't give them license to return to the bondage of the sin they'd been freed from. Using their freedom in order to sin meant allowing their sin to master them. But we are to be mastered by Christ and nothing else.

Peter echoed this message. He said, "Live as free men, but do not use your freedom as a cover-up for evil; live as servants of God" (1 Peter 2:16). As servants of God, we are bound to him. Peter also said that if we lack qualities like self-control, then we are shortsighted and blinded, forgetting our purification from former sin (see 2 Peter 1:9).

This same message was delivered to the Galatians. Paul reminded the Galatians that they were free indeed. But he also told them not to use their freedom to "indulge the sinful nature" (Galatians 5:13). Later, he reminded them that the fruit of the Spirit is self-control. Believing that liberty gives us a license to do anything puts us in a position to be mastered by sin. We combat this tendency by exercising self-control. The logical flow is that I control myself and allow the Holy Spirit to control me.

"I believe the Holy Spirit does convict people differently about different things, so I think it's possible for something

to be a sin for one person and not for another. I also think you have to be in prayer, read the Bible, and ask God to show you if that thing is a sin."   **—Kevin, 17**

So why is it that so many guys pray that the Holy Spirit will give them more self-control over masturbation—and then not get what they prayed for? Maybe he *is* giving it. Self-control may not mean elimination. The range of control can span from not engaging in something at all to regulating it. Paul also illustrated this. He reminded the believer not to be controlled by wine but to be controlled by the Holy Spirit (see Ephesians 5:18).

I know some godly men and women who believe it's wisest to abstain from drinking because of that statement. Their decision certainly is wise. But Paul also advised Timothy to drink a little wine for his stomach (see 1 Timothy 5:23). Timothy had the freedom to control his intake of wine, and this too is wise. Abstinence isn't necessarily wiser than moderation. Control and reliance on the Holy Spirit is wise whether it is played out in a decision to avoid or to regulate.

Some would say that because masturbation can easily master you, the wisest way to avoid this is not to do it at all. That is an option. Others would say that masturbation can easily master you, therefore you should regulate it. Regulation can reveal a repetitive pattern, but that doesn't mean it is mastering the individual.

"If masturbation is a gray issue, I would feel very relieved; I wouldn't feel so guilty."   **—Jarred, 15**

Can masturbation be controlled and engaged in daily? Given the difference in the sexual drives of each individual, and given the conviction and obedience to the Holy Spirit's leading, along with the freedoms we have in Christ, some could answer yes to this question. A universal standard can't be set on control or on freedom. It is the Holy Spirit who becomes the guide. Like any other wisdom issue, masturbation is going to keep us running to, and relying upon, the Holy Spirit. That may be the whole point.

After all, it's possible that God hasn't given us all the answers . . . deliberately. It's also quite possible that God allows some sin to be relative from person to person. Skeptics who want to make all sin universal throw around the biblical phrase "Everyone did what was right in his own eyes" (Judges 21:25, NASB). This is spiritual bullying and ignorance. The relativity of sin regarding wisdom issues doesn't make *all* sin relative. It doesn't give anyone the freedom or right to ignore moral absolutes. Yet God doesn't give us a black-and-white answer to every question we have about an activity's moral quality. In some cases, he creates a "gray zone" that requires us to seek him and his wisdom each day. He tells us this in Proverbs 3:5-6:

> *Trust in the LORD with all your heart and lean not on your own understanding; in all your ways acknowledge him, and he will make your paths straight.*

The Hebrew word for *trust* in this passage means "to be in complete surrender." It's no coincidence that this word abounds in the wisdom literature of Scripture. This verse doesn't just apply to our life plans, though. It applies to the personal issues that we struggle with on a daily basis. It unfolds the process that we must take to discover if something like masturbation is sin for each of us. This issue is gray because Jesus wants us to trust *him*.

The issue is gray because it makes us surrender to him; it makes us bow to Christ, who straightens things out.

Jesus is Lord over the middle.

He is the artist over the gray zone.

He is wisdom personified when I struggle with wisdom issues.

THINK ABOUT IT!

1. What is a "middle issue"? Name some questions of moral behavior that fit into this category for you.

2. To your way of thinking, is masturbation beneficial? Constructive? Mastering? (If you're in a group, take plenty of time to talk this through!)

3. Choose two of the Scripture passages quoted in this chapter that speak most powerfully to your heart. What is the Holy Spirit saying to you, personally, in these words?

4. During the coming week, take some time to memorize the two passages you chose in question three. How will these words help you in your daily walk with God?

5. What does it mean for you, in practical terms, that "Jesus is Lord over the middle"?

CHAPTER EIGHT

PREPARE TO BE LED BY THE HOLY SPIRIT

I wish this guy would just say, "Masturbation is right; knock yourself out" or "Don't be deceived; masturbation is wrong, and you'll burn in hell if you do it."

I think I'm a loving father. I know my children would affirm that. And because I love my kids, I've defined boundaries for them regarding behaviors and values. I don't play guessing games; they know exactly what's expected of them.

It would be cruel of me to tell my kids they have a curfew and that they will be grounded if they violate it, but then make them guess what that curfew time is. Imagine it . . .

"Dad said we'd better not violate our curfew, or else."

"Do you think we'll violate it if we stay out past eight? What about nine? What about one? Maybe we better not go out at all; that's the wisest thing."

"But Dad said we're free to go out! What kind of freedom is this?"

You see, a loving father makes sure the boundaries are defined. My children know their curfew times. They're free to make their decisions and plan their time, as long as they get home by curfew. In other words, *they can enjoy freedom within boundaries.*

But what about the times when a father hasn't defined the boundaries?

WE HAVE A HELPER

After all, any good father will admit he can't have rules for everything. Some boundaries won't be set in concrete. They can be different from one kid to the next, given the heart, will, and specific needs of that child. Because the rules can be fluid, a kid must trust the love of the father. For example, my kids can sit in fear, wondering if they are going to enrage me over the slightest thing that displeases me—or they can run free and trust my love. Out of love I will *discipline* them, not punish them. Get it straight: Discipline means that I'll let them run free and then prompt them, teach them, and guide them when they get too close to the edge.

Sadly, we've been conditioned into thinking that God's desire for us is a bull's-eye and that we have to be in the *center* of it because we're not sure what the expectations are. We don't trust his love. We are free to run, not having to remain standing in the center of the bull's-eye. The Holy Spirit is the prompter. His responsibility is to convict, guide, teach, and be the Helper in our lives. God's *discipline* is constant and loving because he has made us free. He doesn't sit in heaven waiting until we screw up so he can whack us. He gives us great liberty while walking with us.

"The best advice I ever got about masturbation was when a godly friend challenged me to constantly ask the Holy Spirit to control my sexuality. I know when masturbation is sin for me and when it isn't."
— Dan, 21

That's why the Holy Spirit is called "Helper" (see John 14:26; 15:26, NASB). Many times his help and discipline come in the form of an inner conviction. Throughout this book I've been saying that we need to depend on the Spirit. His role in our lives is critical to how we view the issue of masturbation. The Spirit won't play guessing games with us. He has defined some rules, so we won't need to live in fear of judgment. He prompts us regarding wisdom issues so that we can live in freedom.

OBEY WHAT'S CLEAR: SEXUAL PURITY

Before you can decide whether a wisdom issue (specifically masturbation) is sin or not, you have to make sure that you are obeying what's clearly defined in Scripture. Do the math: If you're not obeying the things clearly spelled out, then you won't be discerning about the things that aren't spelled out. Stay constantly in the Word! It specifically says that God's will for his children is their sexual purity. Paul wrote to the Thessalonians:

> *Brethren, we request and exhort you in the Lord Jesus, that as you received from us instruction as to how you ought to walk and please God (just as you actually do walk), that you excel still more. For you know what commandments we gave you by the authority of the Lord Jesus. For this is the will of God, your sanctification; that is, that you abstain from sexual immorality.* (1 Thessalonians 4:1-3, NASB)

Determining if masturbation is a personal sin starts with a commitment to living a sexually pure life. This means you must make Jesus the Lord over your sexuality. He becomes owner and controller of your body. Paul continued to tell the Thessalonians to use their bodies as vessels of honor rather than as vehicles of sinful passion (see verses 4-5). As a vessel of honor, we allow our mind and body to be disciplined and controlled by the Spirit as we set our will upon obedience to him. Paul reminded the Corinthians that their bodies are the dwelling place of the Holy Spirit and that God owns their bodies because he bought (redeemed) them with Christ's blood (see 1 Corinthians 6:19-20).

God's will is that we flee sexual immorality, yet *sexual immorality* is never narrowly defined by any author of Scripture. Even the ancient languages keep that term broad in context. It encompasses many sexual practices and deviances. As a wisdom issue, masturbation could be an issue of sexual immorality but it may not be, as well. We may find that we are being manipulated into putting a lot of time, energy, attention, effort, spiritual fervor, and emotional concentration into an area that matters little to God. If you present your body as a vessel of honor and determine to live sexually pure, the Holy Spirit will give guidance as to whether masturbation is or is not sin (sexually immoral) for you.

Fleeing sexual immorality also means that I allow the Holy Spirit control over my mind. Romans 12:1-2 says,

> *I urge you, brothers, in view of God's mercy, to offer your bodies as living sacrifices, holy and pleasing to God—this is your spiritual act of worship. Do not conform any longer to the pattern of this world, but be transformed by the renewing of your mind. Then you will be able to test and approve what God's will is—his good, pleasing and perfect will.*

The Holy Spirit transforms us by renewing our mind. When determining if masturbation is a sin issue, give the Holy Spirit control over your mind. Many people want to tell us what we should think. I have unfolded a history of misconceptions and lies that have been used to support the premise that masturbation is wrong. God doesn't use deception to support moral principles. He doesn't rely on lies to under-gird his heart and plans on issues of righteousness. He is truth, and he reveals truth. Submission to the Holy Spirit's leading governs a believer's thinking.

Some parachurch leaders confronted me about this. They were concerned that leveling the playing field about the myths of masturbation, and exposing masturbation as a wisdom issue, would confuse some believers who were younger in their faith. They said that teaching about the freedom regarding wisdom issues was great for a more mature believer to wade through, but it seemed irresponsible to allow younger Christians to struggle through this. "They're still requiring the milk of God's Word; they're not ready for the meat!" blurted one guy.

I didn't say this, but I thought, *Wasn't that the same problem the writer of Hebrews was talking about?* That's what the writer of Hebrews said. His readers were *slow to learn*, only taking milk, like babies, when they should have been desiring more solid food. They had *retarded* their learning. The result was that they couldn't discern good and evil (see 5:11-14). Thus, our responsibility is not to tell believers, young or old, what to think, but to urge them to consider their own faith deeply, under the leading of the Holy Spirit.

The problem here, as in so many situations, is that many teachers have developed a "Holy Spirit Complex." Unlike a "Messiah Complex," which makes a person think that he or she is the savior of all, a "Holy Spirit Complex" makes people think they're the convicting agents and discerners of sin in the lives of others. As a result, the learners don't have to put any of their own effort into discerning good and evil. They're just told what they should think. But this, in a sense, intellec-tually enslaves them to somebody else!

So as I was listening to these leaders, I asked why we should start a young, vibrant, passionate believer in bondage and then—only as he or she becomes more mature—challenge that person to be free. That doesn't make sense to me, and it doesn't teach a new believer to rely on the Holy Spirit.

As a matter of fact, Paul stated that if we don't teach freedom, we are false teachers. He warned the Colossians not to be sucked into the doctrine of rules that reflect worldly regulations imposed by leaders who would mandate holy living. He said:

> *Since you died with Christ to the basic principles of this world, why, as though you still belonged to it, do you submit to its rules: "Do not handle! Do not taste! Do not touch!"? These are all destined to perish with use, because they are based on human commands and teachings. Such regulations indeed have an appearance of wisdom, with their self-imposed worship, their false humility and their harsh treatment of the body, but they lack any value in restraining sensual indulgence. (Colossians 2:20-23)*

How is it with you? Perhaps you're having trouble reading this book so far, because you're looking for a specific answer. With the turn of every page, maybe you're thinking, *Hey, I wish this guy would just say, "Masturbation is right; knock yourself out," or "Don't be deceived; masturbation is wrong, and I have no freedom to do it."*

"For me, if it gets to the point where I don't really need to do it, but I do it anyway, then that's out of control."   —Matt, 19

In other words, you've been so conditioned to being *told* what to think that you fear God's wrath when you have to venture into a gray zone. One student told me that he thought he was going to go crazy because he needed someone to tell him what the right thing was. I told him that there is someone who would tell him what is right. My advice was that he obey what's clear in Scripture—the call to sexual purity—and wait patiently and prayerfully on the Holy Spirit.

BE FREE—TO LOVE!

The Galatians wrestled with legalism. Certain teachers tried to add extra requirements to God's plan of salvation by pure grace. Paul wrote to tell them that they were free, but he warned them not to use their freedom as an opportunity to sin. He said that rather than indulging the sinful nature, freedom should be used for a higher purpose: to *love*.

> *You were called to freedom, brothers and sisters; only do not use your freedom as an opportunity for self-indulgence, but through love become slaves to one another. For the whole law is summed up in a single commandment, "You shall love your neighbor as yourself."*
>
> *If, however, you bite and devour one another, take care that you are not consumed by one another. Live by the Spirit, I say, and do not gratify the desires of the flesh. (Galatians 5:13-16, NRSV)*

In verse 14, Paul nicely summarized Jesus' "Great Commandment," from Matthew 22 and Luke 10. So let's turn our thoughts to Jesus for a moment.

He was once approached by a man asking, "What is the greatest commandment?" Now this man was a bottom-line guy. He knew the

Law and all the commands of God, but he was so overwhelmed. He saw an opportunity to ask Jesus to sum it all up. His question can be interpreted as a frustrating plea to Jesus to boil it all down to one thing. He wanted to know *the* most important thing. Jesus told him that the whole Law and the writings of the Prophets could be summarized with this: "'Love the Lord your God with all your heart and with all your soul and with all your mind. . . . [And] love your neighbor as yourself'" (Matthew 22:37-39).

This command has a primary and secondary focus. The first is that we should love God, a vertical relationship. This reverts back to our earlier discussion that we must keep our eyes fixed on Jesus. The goal is to fall in love and keep falling in love with Christ. If you want to have a strong handle on the gray issues, then Jesus has to be the primary love, focus, priority, and pleasure of your life. He must increase, and you must decrease.

By the way, this is a process, not a point at which you suddenly arrive. I've met many precious, godly young men whose hearts line up with this great command and whose lives resonate with a passion to make Christ the highest priority of life. But the Enemy has duped them into believing that they aren't hitting the mark. He lies to them, telling them that loving God is a measurable product or a certain point on a scale. He's defeated them by making them think they don't love God *enough*. In reality, it's a day-by-day process, a progressive, lifelong, non-tedious, exciting lifestyle. There is great freedom in this.

Some have said that masturbation is a form of idolatry because it interferes in a love relationship with God. Because of self-pleasure myths, addiction theories, and guilt and shame, it becomes easy to claim that masturbation is idolatry. The only way it can be idolatry, however, is if you elevate it to a higher place in your life than Jesus.

The one sure way to keep that from happening is *not to be absorbed with the issue by indulging it or eliminating it*. That is, the combat strategy is to focus more on loving Jesus, not on destroying the idols. It's a simple replacement theory. As *he* increases in my life, *he* takes his rightful place as Lord over the lords of my life. *He* deflates, devalues, destroys, and demotes those idols. *He* decides if masturbation is a sin issue, and then *he* gives the victory to embrace or overcome it. *He* replaces the idols. *He* gets the glory because *he* has conquered sin, and then *he* makes us more than conquerors—or, more expressly, he makes us *extreme* conquerors.

The second focus of the Great Commandment is horizontal. Jesus says we should love our neighbors as ourselves. Loving others grows out of loving God. I've seen brothers in Christ become quite heated and angry disputing this issue of masturbation. The debate escalates, voices rise, passions flair, and people walk away wounded. The goal becomes "being right" rather than deepening brotherly love. Yet God hasn't called us to an agenda of rightness. Jesus says people will know we're his disciples by our love for each other (see John 13:34-35).

Let's get specific here: The agenda is not for us to be proved right; the agenda is love. Jesus is clear throughout John 14–16 that it is the Holy Spirit—not you or me—who will lead us into truth. That doesn't mean the truth isn't important, nor does it mean we shouldn't seek, talk about, or stand up for truth. It means that I am not called to convince people of truth no matter what. My calling from God is to live in truth and freedom—and to love.

Over and over again, the Bible tells us just how important love is. Consider a few key passages:

- Love covers sin (see Proverbs 10:12; 1 Peter 4:8).
- Love protects (see Proverbs 20:28).

- Love satisfies God's requirements (see Romans 13:10).
- Love builds up (see 1 Corinthians 8:1).
- Love is patient and kind, not jealous, rude, or demanding (see 1 Corinthians 13:4-5).
- Love bears, believes, hopes in, and endures all things (see 1 Corinthians 13:7).
- Love is the believer's highest goal and priority (see Colossians 2:2; 1 Corinthians 14:1).
- Love shows the Spirit in a believer's life (see Galatians 5:22).
- Love is our armor (see 1 Thessalonians 5:8).
- Love encourages others to do good works (see Hebrews 10:24-25).
- Love expels fear (see 1 John 4:18).
- Love comes from God (see 1 John 4:7).
- Love is the greatest thing (see 1 Corinthians 13:13).

No way is this an exhaustive list! But it certainly drives home the point that our primary objective in all we say and do is: *Love*.

Okay, so how does this relate to masturbation? Well, first—masturbation shouldn't be dividing believers. Romans 14:3 tells us not to have contempt for each other or judge each other over wisdom issues. Each of us must give an account for our personal lives (see Romans 14:12). The Holy Spirit will, in truth, direct each person's conviction in this matter.

Second, if there is freedom to masturbate for some, out of love that person may need to be careful not to flaunt his freedom. He must be aware of the weaker brother and not make that brother stumble (see Romans 14:21). This doesn't mean that we *can* have liberty but we *cannot* exercise it out of fear that someone might learn about us and stumble. If this were true, then there would really be no issues of freedom at all.

Protecting a weaker brother from stumbling means that I must avoid certain practices, or avoid talking about my engagement in certain practices, in the presence of those whom I know to be weaker. (By the way, the weaker brother is the one who thinks he has a handle on truth and does not exercise liberty. They think the person who is engaging in masturbation is the weaker brother because he is engaging in sinful practices. Actually, the opposite is true.)

If God's Word is vague about issues like masturbation, then the Holy Spirit becomes the authority regarding it. The weaker brother is the one who can't see that the debate involves a wisdom issue. Love for the weaker brother mandates that we don't get caught up in heated debates or meaningless quarrels here. It's far better to decide *not* to win with an agenda of rightness. Instead, we can choose to win with the agenda of love.

ACCEPT ACCOUNTABILITY

Despite your personal conclusions about masturbation, you must be accountable. Scripture is clear that there are no lone rangers in the body of Christ. We are to come together to challenge each other to love and do good deeds (see Hebrews 10:24). Proverbs 27:17 says that "as iron sharpens iron, so one man sharpens another." This means that we must challenge each other; we must be accountable for spiritual growth. Don't just gloss over the last three words of that last sentence: *for spiritual growth.* Our ideas of accountability are so bogus because we focus accountability on the wrong things, especially surrounding sexual things.

We give the impressions that accountability happens if intimate secrets and sins are exposed or confessed. So what! While vulnerability and honesty are important, it doesn't make me accountable. The point of accountability is that I enter into an intimate, heart-to-heart relationship that challenges my brother, in a proactive way, to grow spiritually whether we know each other's sin secrets or not.

Some describe their accountability relationship like this: "We sit down and tell each other about our sexual struggles. If my brother is struggling with masturbation, then he calls me, and we pray. If that isn't enough, then I'll drop everything to meet with him so he can win the battle. He does the same for me."

But I don't think it should be like that. To my way of thinking, prayer is the only good part of this idea of accountability; otherwise, it's just an example of codependency. Nobody in this picture is depending on God. Both are conditioning each to depend on the other. Both are fulfilling controlling needs to be needed. No, this is not healthy accountability.

Another kind of accountability makes it into a thoroughly grace-less process. Here's how it works: Two guys get together and share their struggles. If one of the two frequently falls into sin, then the other guy exposes him. This becomes an unsafe and threatening situation. The motivation to stay obedient is *the fear of being shamed*. Most of the time this leads to an impotent accountability relationship because real struggles remain secret and answers to pointed questions are camouflaged with vague, spiritual clichés. This idea of accountability doesn't take love, grace, or protection into account.

The third way I've seen accountability at work is similar to the second. But instead of whacking each other when they fall, both guys come to agreement that this is a problem—and they keep talking, talking, talking about it. This happens because they don't know what to do. Yet it feels good to keep applying the salve of spiritual platitudes to the situation while they hope it goes away.

All of these views demonstrate a remedial approach to accountability. But here's the point: Remedying our problems is the job of the Holy Spirit as we individually surrender to him. Instead of being remedial, suppose we take a *preventive* approach? Then our accountability relationships would focus on helping each other draw closer to God. We'd actively desire to hear what God is teaching our accountability partners. The questions would still be tough ones:

- What is God teaching you these days?
- Where in his Word did he teach you that?
- What in your experiences this week showed God at work?
- How are you applying these things to your life today?
- How is God changing you because of what you've learned?
- Why did God want you to learn that?
- What experiences of God's presence and grace were most powerful for you in the past week or month?
- In what ways are you becoming more aware of God's love for you?

You get the picture. And you could add plenty of your own questions for accountability discussion—questions that put the focus on God's work rather than on your failures.

Let's enter into partnerships to pray together, memorize God's Word together, read and study Scripture together, and do good deeds together. That is how iron sharpens iron. The iron blade becomes dull and rusty when we simply wallow together in a losing battle of willpower or when we meet together for the sole purpose of beating each other up. *Accountability is about developing spiritual disciplines, not about eliminating sinful behaviors.* Wouldn't you like to have an accountability relationship like that?

LET THE HOLY SPIRIT HAVE CONTROL

The apostle James gives us great insight into how to let the Holy Spirit have control over our lives. He says the Spirit jealously desires our full devotion to him (see James 4:5). James then proceeds to give us an outline of some practices that will allow us to give the Holy Spirit free reign. Why not study and memorize James 4:7-10? Here are the steps you'll learn:

1. *Submit to God* (see verse 7). This requires a heart intent on pleasing God. I bow to him. I surrender everything for the greater goal of intimacy with Jesus. I quit fighting, running from, flinching, cowering away from, shamefully hiding from, or opposing God. I submit.

2. *Resist the Devil* (see verse 7). This means that you fight against Satan's deceptions, which make evil things appear acceptable and alluring—or make good things seem corrupt. You recognize that he is a roaring lion who lurks about looking for someone to devour by tempting as well as accusing (see 1 Peter 5:8).

Satan uses shaming guilt as a prime tactic, whereas the Holy Spirit rushes in with a conviction that offers grace and freedom as a way of escape. Satan's tactics also involve getting you to resist God and flee from *him!* Instead, James says that when you resist Satan, Satan will flee from you.

Remember that Satan is responsible for two distinct activities: He *tempts* us to sin and then he *accuses* us of our sin. We tend to forget the second tactic. He accuses to immobilize, defeat, and destroy believers. He takes good things—like morality, medicine, and even Scripture— and twists them out of context.

If we are to formulate a biblical and cultural personal view of masturbation we must realize that much of the residue of the past is built on lies—and Satan is the "father of lies" (John 8:44). Moral, ethical, and supposedly God-honoring ideas were founded on error. This bred a hateful, condemning, and judgmental vocal authority rooted in pagan and Gnostic information about semen conservation, dietary restrictions, and the evil of flesh. They formulated abusive practices, publicly shamed people, and openly exposed anything in opposition to them as heretical. It was no different than the inquisition or the witchhunts of earlier days. All of this falls into the realm of Satan's work to be resisted. (This doesn't make masturbation right, but seeing the foundational lies allows us to level the playing field to formulate a personal view.)

3. *Come near to God* (see verse 8). Shame and defeat keep us from drawing near to God. God never tires of us. His mercy is new every morning. God's love never fails. Romans 8:1 reminds us that there is *no* condemnation to those who are in Christ. (I often wonder what part of *no* we don't understand here!) Not only is there no condemnation, he also continues to love us.

He tells you that nothing can separate you from his love (see Romans 8:35-39). That means his love creates an airtight seal on you. Nothing can separate you from it. You can't even get a piece of paper between you and God's love. By the way, that love is a great love. It is so great that you can confidently know that *God loves you the most*. He loves you with an eternal, immeasurable, unconditional, unfathomable, never-ending love. That's so much that you can't even wrap your mind around it. It is . . . *the most*. He *loves you the most*.

If this is true, which it is, then there's absolutely nothing you can do to affect that love. Masturbation can't separate you from his love. He will not love you less. Get that—let it sink in. *He loves you the most*.

The flip side is true, too. There's nothing that you can do to get more of his love. *He already loves you the most.* Abstaining from masturbating isn't going to gain you more points, give you more favor, or earn you more love in God's eyes. *He loves you the most.* Draw near to him.

4. *Wash your hands and purify your hearts* (see verse 8). James invites us to get our house in order. Cleansing and purifying means that we deal with any known sin in our lives. It's making sure that our relationship with God is tight. As the Holy Spirit reveals sin, we confess our dependence on him and give him control over that area of our lives. Symbolically, it's the act of opening up clean hands before the Lord.

5. *Grieve, mourn, and wail* (see verse 9). This sounds like fun! I thought the Holy Spirit was going to give me joy. Isn't joy part of the fruit of the Spirit? Does this mean that being controlled by the Holy Spirit is a pain?

Yes, he does give joy and *no*, the Spirit's control is not a pain. "Grieve, mourn, and wail" means that as he reveals sin to us, we express our deepest sorrow over it. That is the first step in repentance. It allows me to be a vessel of honor, clean and controlled by him.

6. *Humble yourself before the Lord* (see verse 10). This is an act of complete dependence on God. With regard to wisdom issues, humility means that I admit I don't have a complete lock on the issue. Humility means that in the gray areas, I can't determine right or wrong for anyone else. I am not the standard; my opinion is not authoritative.

Humility means that, ultimately, it doesn't matter whether I am right, and I cease seeking that goal in order to live in more loving ways.

Humility means that I am fine if masturbation is a sin issue or a liberty issue for me, and I'm fine if it is different for another brother. Humility also means that I bow to the Spirit's control; I submit to him. This takes us full circle, back to the beginning of the process: Submit.

The concrete principles are clear. In order to come to a biblically informed personal opinion about masturbation, you must first start by being committed to following God's will of sexual purity, which is for all believers. If you are not on the same page as he is here, then you are already living in sin, and masturbation would be adding fuel to the fire.

Second, be clear that the agenda of the Christian life is love—love for God and love for others. To deviate from this agenda throws the trajectory out of kilter as you deal with any wisdom issue.

Third, form accountability relationships in which you are challenging and being challenged to grow spiritually. "Sharpening" each other means that you are proactive about spiritual disciplines—preventive rather than remedial.

The umbrella over each of these steps is the call to stay in God's Word, day by day. Be all about God's Word. It's the guidebook for keeping you from sin and the sword to protect you in battle. With the Word you'll cut through your sinful attitudes and motives. The Word itself confirms it: "How can a young man keep his way pure? By living according to your word" (Psalm 119:9).

THINK ABOUT IT!

1. In what ways have you experienced the Holy Spirit as *Helper?*

2. What does it mean to you to stay sexually pure? What does this clear calling mean for you when it comes to masturbation?

3. In what ways would you like to be more "free to love"? Have you made this a matter of prayer?

4. What is your experience with accountability relationships? Do you agree that the primary focus should be on spiritual growth rather than sexual struggles? How could that work, in practical terms?

CHAPTER NINE

MAKE YOUR DECISION!

For me and my friends, to masturbate or not to masturbate?
That's the question.

Ashley wasn't shy, so when she and some of her friends met with me, she got right to it: "I heard you're writing a book on masturbation."

"That's right," I said. "You're interested in the topic?"

"Well, actually I'm still trying to decide if it's right or wrong," she said, lowering her voice. "This may sound strange, but I started masturbating as a preteen and never thought it was wrong at all. I didn't even really think of it as sexual, you know?"

"So at that time you had no idea of the controversy surrounding masturbation?"

"Exactly. But as I got into my teens, I started attending a church where they gave everybody the idea it was truly a bad sin. I began to believe that masturbation was wrong for guys—and that it was really, really wrong for girls. You can't believe the guilt and shame I was feeling, Doctor G."

Her friends were nodding as she spoke, giving me the impression they'd-been-there-done-that. I leaned back in my chair, kicked my feet up on my desk, and prepared for a long conversation.

"It was the same all through high school," Ashley was saying. "But then I started to hear there *may not* be a difference in the degree of sin between male and female masturbation. I mean, maybe it's just equal sin. So I started to feel a little relieved, I guess, but I still struggled with a lot of guilt."

"Your thinking changed a little, but your feelings still bothered you?"

"Yeah. And then, when I went away to college, I got involved with this real dynamic church ministry. I had a tight group of friends, and we challenged each other to grow spiritually. We held each other account-able, prayed, loved, and worshiped together. We even talked about sex-ual stuff—the group and our leadership is divided about masturbation. So now I'm hearing it may not be a wrong thing. So, basically, I'm just plain confused: 'To masturbate or not to masturbate? That's the question.'"

And a good question. Each of us must formulate a personal view informed by factual evidence about sexuality and Scripture. But regard-less of your viewpoint, there is freedom: freedom from guilt and shame, freedom to choose to engage or not, and freedom from condemnation. Masturbation, like all other wisdom issues, will provide one of three options for Ashley and for you.

1. You might call it *sinful*, in all cases.

2. You might decide it's an issue of personal *liberty*, within certain boundaries.

3. Or you might see it as requiring continual *discernment*—because at times it may be right and at times it may be wrong.

DECIDING TO CALL IT SIN

You may read through this book and conclude that masturbation is a personal sin issue. This is not at all problematic. The Holy Spirit will reveal exactly what makes masturbation sin for you. Maybe you've connected it with lust. Maybe the Lord is challenging you to be more dependent upon him. Or if masturbation is reinforcing a sinful habit like viewing pornography, then the issue is clear: It would be good for you to stop masturbating. James 4:17 says, "Anyone, then, who knows the good he ought to do and doesn't do it, sins."

Remember that the struggle isn't about shame and condemnation. God loves you the most. Satan would love to make you live in defeat. Christ's death and resurrection has justified you. That means he has put you in a right relationship (an immovable relationship) with God. That has nothing to do with what you do or do not do. He did it all, full and complete.

But will you *do* all the good that you *know?* It's unlikely.

The truth about the Christian life seems to be, however, that no one bats a thousand in facing temptation. As a matter of fact, most of the saints felt that their averages were pretty low. We can improve our performance, and I thank God that this is so. But evidently in this life we will always have occasional experiences of succumbing to temptation. The sad truth is that much of the time I am too weak to resist, and my failure is simply a hard cold fact with which I must live. I have to come to God with the horribly uncomfortable feeling of failure. And finally, with no excuses, I force myself to my knees before him in confession, asking for restoration to a state of usefulness and self-acceptance by his grace. [1]

When you do fall to the sin of masturbation, get up and move on in victory. It's not an unpardonable sin, nor is it a sin that can have any residual affects on you, because God is greater. Realize that there is no condemnation for those in Christ (see Romans 8:1). Paul even rhetorically asks, "Who can condemn you?" He then replies that Christ Jesus, who is the only judge with the authority to condemn you, died for you and is the one who intercedes for you (see Romans 8:34).

How cool is that!

The apostle John takes this a step further because he knew that Satan would love to make you think you are the exception to this "no condemnation" rule. John says that even if *your heart* condemns you, God is greater than your heart (see 1 John 3:20).

The bottom line: Don't allow Satan to let you live in defeat and shame. If you fall, get up and see God's mercy as new. Remember that "he who began a good work in you will carry it on to completion until the day of Christ Jesus" (Philippians 1:6).

If you were to walk out of your house and you tripped and fell, you wouldn't think about not getting up. You wouldn't say, "Oh, I'm such a klutz. I fall down all the time. I'm so sick of this; I'm just going to stay down here." Then for days people would come by and step on you; cars and trucks would drive over you; animals would sniff you and lick your face; and little children would stare and laugh at you. That's ridiculous, because you're not roadkill!

The things that keep you down are the accusations of Satan. He heaps false guilt on you. You can get up and not be roadkill by discerning the difference between conviction, which comes from the Holy Spirit, and false guilt, which comes from Satan.

Conviction is freeing. You will be prompted, reminded, shaken into the realization that what you did was not pleasing to God. The initial feeling is similar to guilt, a sense of sorrow and disappointment—like James 4:9 says—from having compromised your love for God. Conviction allows you the way of freedom, however. You go to God and find him to be a loving Father who is accepting, embracing, and correcting. He fixes it and starts you new again. He gives you strength to continue in victory. He may not eliminate the problem of masturbation, because he knows that it keeps you running to his loving arms.

The end of conviction is always escape, comfort, reconciliation, and freedom. Conviction allows you to see that you are not worthy of the goodness of God but that you are of supreme value to him nonetheless. While you are not *worthy*, you are equally not *worthless*. You are so valuable that Jesus bought you with his blood; you cost the life of God's Son. Conviction marks you as God's child because it comes from the Holy Spirit, who has been set as a seal on your heart.

False guilt, on the other hand, keeps you in the gutter. You feel that sadness and disappointment, but you *don't* run to God. That's the easiest way to do it. "Stay down; you're such a loser," Satan whispers.

"If masturbation is a gray issue, then a lot of people may not struggle with it as much." —Rick, 16

A harder way is for you to feel the sorrow and disappointment and then go to God. Now Satan has to kick it into gear. He starts to accuse you, and you listen. False guilt makes you think that God is getting tired of this and that any day now, he's going to snap with exasperation. When that happens, you're going to get yours, Bucko!

False guilt makes you believe that God is annoyed to no end with you or that he can be exhausted by your screwups. False guilt over masturbation is fueled by many of the misconceptions we uncovered in this book: Your pleasure is wicked and anti-God; your habitual practice is feeding an addiction; your sexual drives and thoughts are always lust.

The end of false guilt is always immobility, frustration, hopelessness, and bondage. False guilt makes you think that you are worthless instead of merely unworthy. It leads you into "stinkin' thinkin'" that devalues, degrades, demoralizes, and diminishes you as a child of the God of the universe and beyond. False guilt makes you diminish the saving and sustaining power of the blood of Jesus Christ. It minimizes his work at Calvary as something that can be overcome. False guilt comes from the vile heart of Satan, disguised as a prompt from God. Yet it embodies deception, destruction, and the death against your spirit.

If masturbation is sin for you, then know the freedom of God through his grace. Know the freedom to struggle against sin. Know that the victory is that you *can* struggle—not that victory is only obtained when you stop masturbating. God's Son has made you free; you are free indeed.

CHOOSING LIBERTY, WITHIN LIMITS

You may have read this book and feel a great weight has been lifted off your shoulders. The Holy Spirit may have taken this opportunity to renew your mind.

I gave a few chapters of this manuscript to a youth pastor friend of mine. He met me at a restaurant to discuss the content, and his response shocked me. He told me that he felt so liberated, because he couldn't believe how many lies he had bought into. He asked the Lord to forgive him for allowing Satan to have that kind of control over his mind. And then he gave the control back to God.

Remember that Romans 14:22-23 says this about a wisdom issue:

> *Whatever you believe about these things [wisdom issues] keep*
> *between yourself and God. Blessed is the man who does not con-*
> *demn himself by what he approves. But the man who has*
> *doubts is condemned if he eats, because his eating is not from*
> *faith; and everything that does not come from faith is sin.*

Paul was telling the Romans that they had the liberty to eat meat, even though some believers wavered, wondering if it was right or wrong. They were failing to seek the conviction of the Holy Spirit, who would solidify their views regarding the wisdom issue. They were not acting on faith. Paul said that that was a no-brainer sin.

So you've prayed and submitted to the Holy Spirit, and you've allowed him to control your thinking. And you feel that masturbation is not a sin issue. Then, by your faith, determine it not to be sin for you. If you ask the Holy Spirit to take away the desire and need to masturbate, and he doesn't, and you conclude that he is changing your heart and mind, then seek him some more. If you pray and he doesn't change things, then trust that he has answered you.

Act in faith.

Remember, you may be putting too much emotional, intellectual, and spiritual energy into something that matters little to God.

"As I started to pray about this issue more, I discovered more freedom with it." —Dan, 21

Paul also reminds you in the previous verses that if you find freedom to masturbate, then that freedom is between you and God. Don't give in to those who attempt to universalize masturbation as wrong. Don't compromise your convictions or your freedom.

On the other hand, don't flaunt your freedom. Quietly keep this as an issue between you and God. Remember that your love for God and your love for your brother mark you as a disciple. It is not worth the energy of the debate, especially if your brother is rigid in his conviction. Be the stronger brother. Remind him that you will give an account to God and you are secure in that. Then change the subject and talk about the goodness of God! (Also remember that your love for God becomes the highest priority and the motivator for all you do in life. Loving him becomes the pleasure of all pleasures.)

The last thing that you must remember, if you find freedom in masturbation, is that your liberty should not be license to sin. Freedom has boundaries. If masturbation is reinforcing some other sin, then you are using your freedom wrongly. Instead, constantly be seeking and submitting to the control of the Holy Spirit, even if you have liberty in masturbation.

Continued control by the Spirit will make the free man aware of when he is being mastered by something. Masturbation must be controlled just like eating, drinking, recreation, and so on. If you have liberty to masturbate, put personal checks and balances on it so that you can keep it under control. One student told me that when he came to the realization that he had freedom to masturbate, there wasn't as much tension. He said that he was able to control the frequency and intensity. For him, masturbation was okay once or twice a week. He limited it so he wouldn't be mastered by it.

DISCERNING THE RIGHT AND WRONG TIMES

I've met many guys who've concluded that masturbation is right for them at times and in certain circumstances — and wrong at other times.

These young men have come to know exactly when their minds cross the line between lust and God-given sexual thought. They don't feel the need or desire to masturbate impulsively.

Many times these men view masturbation as a way of escape from sexual sin. They masturbate to avoid falling into greater sexual temptation. When challenged by the question of "Can't God deliver you without masturbation?" they confidently conclude that, in fact, God can and does deliver them *through* masturbation. They believe strongly that masturbation is a God-given gift.

Some of these men find it appropriate to masturbate before a date. They may feel that masturbation is appropriate for them in the context of marriage when they're separated from their spouse on business trips. During masturbation, these married guys often restrict their thoughts to recalling marital sexual experiences.

Regardless of the reasons, there are some to whom the Holy Spirit gives very specific direction. He doesn't give a blanket of liberty nor does he give a blanket of restraint.

So how does the Romans 14:22-23 passage work here? Aren't these persons wavering? Not at all. They are staying within the boundaries of freedom. Their conviction is very specific, and they act in faith and confidence.

I understand this principle because I worked for a school where the members of the faculty were required to be an example to students with regard to alcohol. Faculty members were strongly encouraged not to drink in the presence of students, and they were forbidden to drink with students. Many faculty members decided that if they were to have a drink, they would only do it when they were out of town and not near the school or students. Their convictions defined when the issue was appropriate and when it was not.

There is no difference with the issue of masturbation. The questions surrounding it make us depend more on God. It is an issue that requires us to make an informed personal decision. It is an issue that should be accompanied by freedom, regardless of personal view.

So, enough said? I do pray that this book brings you freedom. Because of Christ's great love, you are free from the shame and false guilt that can accompany masturbation. You are free from the bondage that comes with silence and judgment from past and present opinions. You are free from the tyranny and terror created by false teachers who have twisted Scripture to support their dogmatic views.

You are free to be fully sexual and know that it is pure. You are free from Satan's temptations and accusations. You are free to run to God and find him always loving you the most. You are free to *live* victoriously because you *are* victorious. You are free to engage or not engage in masturbation. You are free to struggle—during the struggle, and from the struggle.

God's Son has made you free—You are free!

THINK ABOUT IT!

1. Of the three options discussed in this chapter, which is most likely to be your personal conclusion about masturbation? Why?

2. If masturbation is sin for you, how do you plan to avoid wallowing in guilt or shame should you "slip up"?

3. If you have liberty with masturbation, what kinds of boundaries will you set for yourself?

4. To what extent has the idea of "freedom in Christ" become deeply real for you? How can you make it more of a practical, day-by-day reality?

5. What one or two key principles do you want to remember from your readings in this book? How will you apply them to your life in the coming days?

VICTORIAN ERA SYMPTOMS

The Victorian era viewed masturbation as the cause of virtually every adolescent health problem. Among the diseases and disorders produced by "self-abuse" were:

mental illness
schizophrenia
extreme paranoia
depression
anxiety
hysterics
hypochondria
loss of memory
any acute learning disability, including idiocy and stupidity
antisocial behaviors
shyness and timidity
epilepsy
convulsions
sensory impairments, such as loss of sight, hearing, taste, and smell
weakness
chronic fatigue and loss of energy
lethargy
nervous disorders
dizziness and fainting spells
disorientation
chronic insomnia or constant drowsiness
fevers and headaches
rheumatism
skeletal disorders ranging from stunted growth to gout

muscular disorders, including paralysis
numbness and frequent painful spasms
cardiovascular disorders, including hypertension
palpitations and heart failure
gastrointestinal problems, including nausea
stomachaches
choking
constipation
diarrhea and hemorrhoids
skin problems ranging from acne to rashes
skin lesions
paleness or pigment discoloring
dark circles under the eyes
baldness and premature whitening of the hair
respiration problems, including coughing spells
asthma and tubercular consumption
venereal diseases, such as gonorrhea
burning upon urination
disorders of the genitalia, such as cysts, tumors, infections, or pain

Stengers and Van Neck in their book *Masturbation: The History of a Great Terror* show a series of 16 illustrations that were distributed in a propaganda pamphlet and used in medical classrooms, of a 17 year old afflicted with the deadly vice of masturbation. The illustrations start with a healthy looking young man and show a progressive degeneration to the point of death. Each picture give a description of the symptom and affliction that rapidly overtakes a masturbator. These pictures are based on Tissot's account of the patients that he treated.

Some authorities even believed that masturbation might lead to criminal behavior and homosexuality. Ultimately, if masturbation wasn't caught and exposed in time, the outcome was death.

PREVENTIONS FROM THE PAST

The authoritative figures of the last two or three centuries believed they had a handle on truth regarding masturbation. They believed they were working on God's behalf to rid the world of this disgusting, revolting, loathsome, vile, self-polluting, self-abusing, unnatural, disease-producing (the list can go on) vice. Their message was so urgent because of the presumed impending divine judgment. Therefore, they concocted many preventions and cures.

Some of the preventions and cures, like nutritional changes to diet, were mild. Other measures were more severe. For example, it was believed that boys should not be left alone for long periods of time because of what they might do to themselves. Thus, elaborate exercise plans were established. It was believed that sports could deter sexual energies (a false view that is still held today). Boys were run through rigorous programs for the intended purpose of fatiguing them in the hope that they'd fall fast asleep and not masturbate in bed. Certain childhood activities, such as climbing a rope or sliding down banisters, were forbidden because they could cause arousal.

Programs were designed to minimize arousal and erection. Students were required to read wholesome literature to divert their minds from sexual ideas. Literature was screened for themes to be avoided, like romance, because such reading might evoke passion or give rise to thoughts of sensual pleasure. Students were encouraged to memorize long poems on morals when the urge to masturbate overtook them.

Physicians would recommend diminishing the amount of liquid that the individual consumed before bedtime. It was even believed that contact with the genitals should be minimized during washing and urination. One text says that urination should be done quickly, and that shaking the penis should be avoided, even if it meant that urine would get into one's pants.

Some of these practices are still recommended today. I recently ran across an article online entitled "Overcoming Masturbation: A Guide to Self Control." It is written by a leader in the Mormon church and is distributed to men at Brigham Young University. Some of the tips include:

- leaving the bathroom door or shower curtain partly open to discourage being alone during toilet and shower activities.
- taking cool, brief showers.
- keeping the bladder empty and refraining from drinking large amounts of fluids before retiring.
- reducing the amount of spices and condiments in food.
- wearing pajamas that are difficult to open.
- tying hands to the bedposts if masturbation is severe.[1]

Others decided to market preventive methods, ranging from powders and elixirs to devices designed to be worn by the individual. These devices included forms of chastity belts in which the penis was inserted and allowed urine to pass. The belt was locked on, insuring that the penis couldn't be excited by touch or other stimulation. Other devices included penis rings containing metal spikes that would pierce the penis if erection occurred, special school benches that wouldn't allow boys to cross their legs, and abdominal straitjackets that wrapped the genitalia so that the individual wearing the jacket couldn't remove it.

Some investigative research would reveal that there are a myriad of patents issued by the U.S Patent Office for anti-masturbatory devices. Some of these patents were issues as late as the 1930's although the majority were issued before the turn of the century. These devices included various types of cages and metal sheaths that would prevent the wearer from handling his genitals. Other devices included various forms of trusses that kept young men from having erections by painfully pulling and tying the wearer's penis to his leg. If erection began, the penis did not have any room to vasocongest, making the experience painful. Another category of devices were tumescence response devices. These anti-masturbatory apparatuses worked by triggering levers when the girth and length of the penis changed with erection. The levers would administer anything from ice water to electrical shock.

Parents were even encouraged to tie their children's hands and feet to the bedposts at night to keep them from touching themselves or rubbing against the bed while they slept. Some devices set off alarms if the child began to move in bed. The bells warned parents that their child may be masturbating or having a wet dream. In any case, the alarm signaled the parent to douse the child with cold water that was kept near the bed!

If these methods didn't cure the masturbator, then other, more extreme, methods were employed. Some doctors recommended that the penis or clitoris of excessive masturbators be cauterized. This process involved cutting and burning the penis or clitoris, killing nerve endings and creating scar tissue so that the organ wasn't as sensitive to pleasure. Women could have the clitoris removed entirely. And for men, in extreme cases, the penis was castrated to keep the severe masturbator from death.

TIPS FOR PARENTS AND YOUTH WORKERS

A NOTE TO PARENTS

1. Recognize that the issue of masturbation is a wisdom issue. The controversy that this book will generate will rise and fall on a person's perspective about this point. Scripture does not directly address this issue but it does address almost every other sexual issue. This is strong evidence that the issue of masturbation is a wisdom issue. What does that mean? Basically, it could be sin for some and not for others.

The New Testament deals with many wisdom issues. The church through the ages has followed suit in how it continues to deal with them. Our task is to teach our children to make biblical and God-honoring decisions about these issues. Throughout this book I have taken a neutral stance, although some may say that I haven't because of my "sacred-cow tipping." When dealing with wisdom issues, we must expose the lies that have been used in supporting a false view. Hopefully, this book levels the playing field.

A long, intense look at the history of views on masturbation reveals that the foundational theories were built on ignorance, deception, and dogmatic opinions regarded as truth. These foundational theories gave rise to a moral panic that occurred, particularly in the mid-nineteenth century and around the turn of the twentieth century. Regardless of one's personal conviction on the issue of masturbation, it would be difficult to dismiss the gross errors that grew out of this era. These errors not only created a terror over masturbation specifically, and sexuality in general, but generated a fear for loss of life and an incredible sense of shame.

2. *Don't be deceived: Ignoring this as a wisdom issue is deceptive.* What if you were to teach something that is sin as being acceptable? You'd be called a false teacher. Let's rephrase the question a bit: What if you were to teach something as sin that is not sin? You still wind up as a false teacher. To teach something as sin that is *not* sin is equally false teaching as to teach something that *is* sin as being acceptable. Christ's finished work on Calvary insures our freedom. Satan desires to rob us of that in any strategic way that he can. Buying into his lies and bondage on either side of a wisdom issue is not a delight to God.

We must remember that Satan is responsible for two distinct activities: He tempts us to sin and then he accuses us of our sin. The first we understand because we know how he takes evil things and makes them look very attractive. We tend to forget the second. He accuses to immobilize, defeat, and destroy believers. He takes good things like presented morality, medicine, and even Scripture and twists them out of context. I am not saying that masturbation is good, nor am I saying that it is bad. If we are to help young people formulate a biblical and personal view of masturbation we must realize that much of the thought from the past is built on lies. Many moral, ethical, and supposedly God-honoring ideas were founded on error.

This bred a hateful, condemning, and judgmental vocal authority informed from pagan and Gnostic roots about semen conservation, dietary needs, and the evil of flesh. They formulated abusive practices, publicly shamed people, and openly exposed anything in opposition to them as heretical in a style similar to the Inquisition or the witchhunts of earlier days. This fact doesn't make masturbation right, but seeing the foundational lies allows us to level the playing field to formulate a personal view.

3. *Wisdom issues are a part of the Christian life so that we continuously run to and trust God for our answer.* God's Word is clear on this matter. We shouldn't trust our own understanding; rather we should place our trust in him and he'll direct us (see Proverbs 3:5-6). Wisdom issues make us run to God, not rest in the shallow, impotent, pat answers passed down by tradition. We need to teach our children to test teaching to see if it is from God (see 1 John 4:1). Follow this simple pattern when dealing with wisdom issues:

- Search and study Scripture: Dig in and study passages that correlate to this issue. God's Word promises to be light and guide us away from sin (see Psalm 119:9-11,105).

- Survey Satan's strategy: Realize that his tactics involve temptation and accusation. We know about the temptation part but we fail to discern that shame is the by-product of his accusation. He wants to shut down the believer. Also remember that he deceives by making evil things appear good and good things appear evil. Yet a wisdom issue may not be an evil thing for some believers.

- Seek the wisdom of godly men and women: Don't just swallow what teachers say. Nobody plans to be a false teacher and even the most godly teacher can be deceived. Yet Scripture is clear that there is wisdom in the counsel of many godly men and women (see Proverbs 11:14; 12:15; 15:22; 19:20-21; 24:6). Listen and discern their teaching and advice. (By the way, this issue of masturbation has many godly men and women lined up on both sides of it.)

- Submit and be sensitive to the Holy Spirit: We forget that the same Holy Spirit that lives and leads in our lives and in the lives of godly leaders is the same Holy Spirit that lives, leads, teaches, and works in the lives of our kids. He constantly points us to truth. He continuously glorifies Christ. We need to teach our kids to be dependent on him for answers, not dependent on us. If we always tell our kids what to think and resolve all the issues for them, they will never know the tension and joy of trusting him. Push your kids into the teaching arms of the Holy Spirit.

- Stand firm and free: Teach your kids to be confident in their decisions about wisdom issues, as Paul taught the Romans. Teach them the boundaries surrounding wisdom issues. Teach them how to love the weaker brother and glorify Jesus Christ. Teach them how to live free.

4. *Parents, give your children peace of mind:*

- Warn them that they will hear conflicting opinions about this issue. There is not a right or wrong truth to the issue of masturbation.

- Allow them to understand that they are normal if masturbation has happened or is happening. This is particularly important for dads (or a significant male) to tell their preteen boys. It is also important to explain how ejaculation works. Explain it in positive terms; after all, God designed it good. Explain that it is a good feeling. Explain what ejaculation is and what it looks like. This will minimize the trauma and embarrassment that a kid might experience.

- Open the door of discussion. Start the conversation by saying that *you* need to talk about this because *you* want your young person to hear your heart on this issue. Assume that your kid has probably heard something about the issue of masturbation, but don't be surprised if he or she has not.

- Avoid putting your kid on the spot for an answer. Try not to ask questions. This often puts a young person on the defense. Share some things that you think are important about the issue of masturbation. You might want to say something like, "I know that you'll hear all sorts of things about masturbation. I just want to tell you some things that I think about it." Then don't push for a response. Remember, you are working to create an open and safe environment. While your kid may not be talking to you, he or she is listening.

- Be honest about the comfort level. Acknowledge that this may be a difficult subject to talk about as much as it is to listen to. Tell your kid that many parents would never talk about this issue with their children because it's uncomfortable, but that you are doing it because you value him or her enough to get past the discomfort.

- Don't overtalk the issue. Whet their appetites to want to know more. Guide them in the way that they should go (see Proverbs 22:6).

A NOTE TO YOUTH WORKERS

Youth workers, you play a critical role in the life of a teenager regarding this issue. Your silence will communicate as much as your words. Speak up, but speak wisely. Many students will talk to you about this issue because they feel uncomfortable talking to their parents. There are some important tips that you should remember as well:

1. *Be careful not to make your opinion scriptural truth.* Own your opinions and share them. If masturbation is sin *for you,* say it that way; if it is not, say it that way as well. Remind them that there are very godly men and women who line up on various points of the opinion spectrum regarding masturbation. Responsible shepherding demands that you send the student on a quest to find the Holy Spirit's direction for his or her life.

2. *Coach parents.* Many parents don't know what to say about this issue. You can recommend that parents follow the same criteria that you will challenge their kids to follow. That criterion is to seek the Lord in matters of wisdom. Organize a "parents only" discussion group around critical issues. Challenge the pat answers by asking parents to explain what they mean. You may be helping many parents formulate a biblical and personal view—for the first time. The struggle over masturbation does not just involve dealing with the act of masturbation. It is a struggle to formulate a godly view, a struggle of renewing our minds, a struggle over having God-honoring conversations about a sensitive issue. It is a struggle to know what and how to teach and then to let God be in control of the hearts and minds of our kids regarding sexual issues.

3. *Get your volunteers on the same page.* The point of agreement on the issue of masturbation should be that you and your staff will commit to training kids to run to the Lord with this issue.

- Make sure that your staff differentiates between their opinions and the authority of Scripture.

- Teach them to avoid judgmental and shaming comments. Work hard to combat the blanket of shame that has covered the church regarding this issue.

- Remember that you can still hold to the opinion that masturbation is wrong *for you*, without it being a universal sin issue and a shaming experience for all.

4. *Use this book as a small-group discussion guide with high school guys.* One youth pastor has taken this book and walked his small group through it. He said that it generated great discussion about a number of issues and forced the group to become more sensitive to the Holy Spirit's teaching. He commented that the guys in the group felt a great sense of relief just over the fact that they became aware that they were not alone in their struggle.

Then, after studying this subject, you may want to use this to generate further study on topics like freedom in Christ; the work of the Holy Spirit in the believer's life; understanding Satan's work and strategy; sexual purity and lust; dealing with other wisdom issues; and so on.

NOTES

CHAPTER 1

1. Stephen Arterburn and Fred Stoeker, *Every Young Man's Battle* (Colorado Springs, Colo.: Waterbrook Press, 2002), p. 115.

CHAPTER 2

1. S. A. Tissot, *Onanism: Or a Treatise upon the Disorders Produced by Masturbation,* as reprinted in Randolph Trumbach, *Marriage, Sex, and the Family in England 1660-1800: A Forty-Four Volume Facsimile Series* (New York: Garland Publishing, 1985), pp. 4-5. Tissot also notes that this disorder, with the symptoms as described in chapter 2, became commonly known as Hippocrates' Second Dorsal Consumption. Tissot argued that masturbation brought on this disorder.

2. John D. Woodbridge, ed., *Great Leaders of the Christian Church* (Chicago, Ill.: Moody Press, 1988), pp. 86, 88.

3. See Thomas Aquinas, *Summa Theologica.* Aquinas refers to masturbation as vitium contra naturam or a "sin against nature" which is a "pollution . . . provoked to obtain sexual pleasure."

4. Bruce King, *Human Sexuality Today,* 4th ed. (Upper Saddle River, N.J.: Prentice Hall, 2002), p. 329; Vern Bullough and Bonnie Bullough, *Sexual Attitudes: Myths and Realities* (Amherst, N.Y.: Prometheus Books, 1995), p. 67. Bullough and Bullough believe that the Greek translation was more accurately translated to mean "arousing the genitals."

5. Felix Podimattam, *A Difficult Problem in Chastity: Masturbation* (Bangalore, India: Asian Trading Corporation, 1973), p. 21.

6. Jean Stengers and Anne Van Neck, *Masturbation: The History of a Great Terror* (New York: Pelgrave, 2001), p. 20.

7. John Money, *The Destroying Angel: Sex, Fitness and Food in the Legacy of Degeneracy Theory, Graham Crackers, Kellogg's Corn Flakes and American Health History* (Buffalo, N.Y.: Prometheus Books, 1985), p. 45. Money sees this as being the momentum for the church to begin its hunt on masturbators, paralleled to witch-hunting.

8. Onania: The heinous sin of self-pollution and all its frightful consequences, in both sexes considered, with spiritual and physical advice to those who have already injured themselves by this abominable practice; and seasonable admonition to the Youth of the Nation (of both sexes) and those whose tuition they are under, whether parents, guardians, masters, or mistresses, 4th ed. (1718), p. 19.

9. Tissot, p. 2.

10. Tissot, as quoted by Stengers and Van Neck, p.7.

11. See King, p. 329.

12. Tissot, p. 24.

13. Tissot, p. 25.

14. Money, pp. 17-19.

15. Bullough and Bullough, p. 71.

16. A Medical Dictionary (London, 1745), as quoted by Stengers and Van Neck, p. 56.

17. Leslie Hall, "Forbidden by God, Despised by Men: Masturbation, Medical Warnings, Moral Panic, and Manhood in Great Britain, 1850-1950," Journal of the History of Sexuality, vol. 2, no. 3 (1992); as reprinted in John Fout, Forbidden History: The State, Society and the Regulation of Sexuality in Modern Europe (Chicago: University of Chicago Press, 1990), p. 294.

18. See Stengers and Van Neck. These authors carefully document a number of medical journals, dictionaries, and encyclopedias from the Victorian era that emphatically state masturbation to be the direct cause of disease. Leslie Hall, in the article "Forbidden by God," also documents medical writings from prominent and influential physician educators that held to this premise.

19. David Gordon, Self-Love (Baltimore, Md.: Penguin, 1968). Gordon talks about how doctors "swooped down" on their patients because they believed that they could see the evidence of masturbation. Their goal was to solicit confession.

20. Dr. J. B. DeBourge (1860), as quoted in Stengers and Van Neck, p. 3.

21. Dr. C. F. Vent, Satan in Society (Cincinnati: Edward F. Hovey Publishers, 1870).

22. Dr. Reveille-Parise (1828), as quoted in Stengers and Van Neck, p. 3.

23. Dr. Reveille-Parise.

24. Money, p. 24.

25. J. H. Kellogg, Plain Facts for Young and Old (Burlingame, Iowa: I. F. Senger, 1882), pp. 332-344, as quoted by Bullough and Bullough, p. 75.

26. See Wilhelm Stenkle, Auto-Eroticism: A Psychiatric Study of Onanism and Neurosis (New York: Liveright Publishing Corporation, 1950). Stenkle examines masturbation as it relates to many correlating issues. The entire book is composed of various case studies from patients who he treated. Many of the men and women in his studies suffered from fear, defeat, suicidal ideation, and so on because they bought into

the myths and misconceptions developed in earlier eras. These myths had been passed down to the patient from friends, parents, or other authorities.

27. *Handbook for Boys*, (published by Boy Scouts of America), as quoted by Gordon, p. 24.

CHAPTER 3

1. B. Zilbergeld, *Male Sexuality* (Boston: Little, Brown, 1978), p. 138. Zilbergeld cites that masturbation is often less preferable than intercourse and more commonly practiced by people who are without partners.

2. Studies by H. Leitenberg, J. Detzer, and D. Srebnik, "Gender differences in masturbation and the relation of masturbation experience in preadolescence and/or early adolescence to sexual behavior and sexual adjustment in young adulthood," *Archives of Sexual Behavior* 22 (1993) pp. 87-98, and a study done by Hurlbert and Whittaker, "The role of masturbation in marital and sexual satisfaction: A comparative study of female masturbators and non-masturbators," *Journal of Sex Education and Therapy* 17 (1991) pp. 272-282, show that masturbation prior to and during marriage has a correlation to a higher degree of marital and sexual satisfaction. S. McCammon, D. Know, and C. Schacht, *Choices in Sexuality* (St. Paul, Minn.: West Publishing Company, 1993), p. 340, report that women who masturbate are better able to teach their partners what pleasures them. This often leads to a more satisfying relationship. There are many more studies that show that masturbation is beneficial to helping couples overcome sexual issues and dysfunction, leading to more satisfying relationships.

3. Dr. Erwin Lutzer, *Ten Lies About God and How You Might Already Be Deceived* (Nashville: Nelson, 2000).

4. James B. Nelson, *The Intimate Connection* (Philadelphia: Westminster, 1988), as quoted in Gary Wilde, *Integrity: Character Counts* (Wheaton, Ill.: Victor, 1996), p. 41.

5. Lutzer, p. 165.

6. Words to "Draw Me Close," by Kelly Carpenter, copyright 1994 Mercy/Vineyard Publishing; ASCAP.

CHAPTER 4

1. Friedrich vonHardenberg, *The Columbia World of Quotations* (Columbia University Press, 1996), from Bartleby.com.

2. S. McCammon and D. Know, et. al., *Choices in Sexuality* (St. Paul, Minn.: West Publishing Company, 1993), p. 334.

3. *Gale Encyclopedia of Medicine.* See the website at www.findarticles.com/cf_dls/g2601/0011/2601001125/p1/article.jhtml

4. Ronald Rolheiser, *The Holy Longing: The Search for a Christian Spirituality* (New York: Doubleday, 1999), p. 5.

CHAPTER 5

1. This was not written as law until Moses wrote the Torah ("the Law") hundreds of years later. It was a part of the traditional, customary expectations of the family of Abraham. Moses includes this in the Law as recorded in Deuteronomy 25:5-10. The term levirate comes from the Latin, meaning "husband's brother." In the Law, if the husband's brother does not perform his duty to preserve his brother's name so that it is "not . . . blotted out from Israel" (Deuteronomy 25:6), then he would be publicly disciplined.
2. Leon, Morris, *Tyndale New Testament Commentaries: 1 Corinthians* (Leichester, England: InterVarsity, 1999).
3. Hans Dieter Betz, *The Sermon on the Mount* (Minneapolis, Minn.: Fortress Press, 1995), pp. 231-235.

CHAPTER 6

1. C. S. Lewis, *Mere Christianity* (New York: Touchstone Books, 1996), pp. 90-91.
2. Frederick Buechner, *Wishful Thinking: A Theological ABC* (San Francisco: HarperSanFrancisco, 1973), p. 65.
3. James E. Dittes, *The Male Predicament: On Being a Man Today* (San Francisco: Harper and Row, 1985).
4. Lewis, p. 94.

CHAPTER 7

1. *Babbette's Feast*, Gabriel Axel, director, Denmark: Panorama Production Company, 1987.

CHAPTER 9

1. Keith Miller, *Habitation of Dragons* (Grand Rapids, Mich.: Baker, 1993), p. 150.

APPENDIX B

1. Mark E. Petersen, *Council of the 12 Apostles,* "Overcoming Masturbation: A Guide to Self Control," (http://Nowscape.com/mormon/mormast.htm).

AUTHOR

DR. STEVEN GERALI has over twenty-five years of experience in youth ministry and the field of adolescent development. Based in southern California, he has conducted seminars and workshops for groups all across North and South America and Europe.

Read, Think, Pray, Live
A guide to reading the bible in a new way
Tony Jones
1-57683-453-0

Learn to meet Jesus in a new way by using an effective study technique that's been used by Christians since the Middle Ages.

The Message Remix
Eugene H. Peterson
Hardback
1-57683-434-4
Bonded Alligator Leather
1-57683-450-6

With added verse-numbered paragraphs and new intros, this book will help a new generation get into God's Word.

Posers, Fakers, & Wannabes
Unmasking the Real You
Brennan Manning and Jim Hancock
1-57683-465-4

As much as we try, we'll never fool God with the games we play or the masks we wear. The best part is: We don't need to. The Father already knows and accepts us exactly as we are.